HOW YOU
CAN BE
A PEACEMAKER

How You Can Be a Peacemaker

Catholic Teachings and Practical Suggestions

Mary Evelyn Jegen, SND

LIGUORI
PUBLICATIONS

One Liguori Drive
Liguori, Missouri 63057
(314) 464-2500

Imprimi Potest:
John F. Dowd, C.SS.R.
Provincial, St. Louis Province
Redemptorist Fathers

Imprimatur:
+ Edward J. O'Donnell
Vicar General, Archdiocese of St. Louis

ISBN 0-89243-231-4
Library of Congress Catalog Card Number: 84-52885

Each of the chapters in this book was originally published by Liguori in pamphlet form. In the order in which they appear here, the pamphlet titles are: (1) *The Teaching of Jesus on Love and Nonviolence*; (2) *John Paul II: Pope of Peace*; (3) *Nuclear Weapons: What Does the Church Teach?*; (4) *To Reach Peace, Teach Peace*; (5) *What Should I Teach My Child About War?*; (6) *Bombs and Bread: Can We Have Both?*; (7) *Four Ways You Can Help Hungry People.*

The author's Introduction in this book first appeared as a contribution in the book PEACEMAKERS: *Christian Voices in the New Abolitionist Movement*, edited by Jim Wallis. It is reprinted here with permission of Harper & Row, publishers.

Dedication

For Eileen Egan
peacemaker and friend

About the Author

Mary Evelyn Jegen, a Sister of Notre Dame, has been an educator all of her adult life. She has taught on the elementary, high school, and university levels in the United States and in Rome.

As the first executive director of the Bread for the World Educational Fund from 1976 to 1978, she designed an interdisciplinary program on world hunger that continues to be used in hundreds of colleges.

One of the establishers of the U.S. branch of Pax Christi, the international Catholic peace movement, Sister Mary Evelyn served as national coordinator from 1979 through 1982. Currently, she is the U.S. representative on the Pax Christi International Human Rights Commission, and was elected vice-president of Pax Christi International in 1984. She also has chaired the national council of the American Fellowship of Reconciliation, an interfaith peace movement.

Sister has a Ph.D. in medieval history from St. Louis University. She lectures extensively on peace issues, and has contributed numerous articles on various peace topics. Her major research interest in recent years has been the transformation of the human meaning of war; the international review *Concilium* has published her study entitled "An Entirely New Attitude."

Contents

Foreword

Sister Mary Evelyn Jegen has a message of extraordinary importance. She speaks to a moment which the Catholic bishops of the United States call "a moment of supreme crisis." The arms race poses a threat to human life and human civilization which is without precedent. (*The Challenge of Peace: God's Promise and Our Response. A Pastoral Letter on War and Peace*)

My experience as one of the members of the National Conference of Catholic Bishops was to set for myself three criteria in the writing of that pastoral letter. I said to myself: This document must be basically *scriptural*; secondly, this document must be *prophetic*; and finally, this document must be *a call to action*. I find all three of those criteria fulfilled in this book.

It is *scriptural*. Every chapter and every page reverberate with the Gospel message of Jesus. This book affirms that Jesus Christ is the source of peace: "Peace I bequeath to you, my own peace I give you, a peace the world cannot give, this is my gift to you." (John 14:27) Especially significant is the link between peace and the practice of the spiritual and corporal works of mercy.

It is *prophetic*. The power that prevails in this book is the deep conviction of the prophetic. It begins with the prophets of the Old Testament (Jeremiah, Isaiah, Micah, etc.) and the disciples of the New Testament (Stephen, Peter, Paul, John, etc.). It continues with our modern-day prophets (Dorothy Day, Martin Luther King, Mahatma Gandhi, etc.) and the great array of those who are following in their footsteps. Sister Mary Evelyn shows us the features of that prophetic destiny.

It is *a call to action*. Too many of us are spectators. Because of the complexity of the issues we do nothing. We are content to be silent. We must become aware that there are not only sins of commission, there are also sins of omission. Not to be involved and not to take action is to be renegade to one's calling as a Christian. Sister Mary Evelyn by voice and by example issues a clarion call to do something: "Learn and Act." These are her words.

This book fulfills the three basic requirements of being scripturally based, prophetically stated, and a call to action. But permit me to state four reasons why I believe you will find this book helpful to you personally and to the Church whose member you are. I believe firmly that everything we do in the Church today should follow the model of the catechumenate. This requires that we have a fourfold ministry — in this instance, a fourfold ministry to peace. I see this book as an exemplary following of this RCIA model given to us in the Catholic bishops' pastoral on education entitled *To Teach as Jesus Did*. Permit me to explain these four ministries to peace:

1. Message. As you read this book you will quickly realize that Sister Mary Evelyn is by disposition a teacher. A number of chapter headings speak of the teachings of Jesus, the teaching of children, the teaching of peace, etc. Especially appropriate, it seems to me, is the teaching on love and nonviolence. More and more important in the days ahead will be the teaching on nonviolent civilian-based defense. Alternatives to violence must more and more occupy our attention. There are countless references to the teachings of the Church. Many quotes are attributed to John XXIII, Paul VI, and John Paul II. Within the next few years we will see an ever-expanding development of the doctrine of peace. I foresee a return to the early pacifist tradition of the Church. In my lifetime more than 60,000,000 people have been killed in wars. Love must overcome violence.

10

2. Community. If I were to pick out one word of great significance it would be the word *interdependence*. We cannot live isolated and alone, whether as persons or as nations. Sister Mary Evelyn will help us to reach a new plateau in our thinking. While upholding and appreciating our Declaration of Independence of 1776, we must raise our sights and begin to implement a Declaration of Inter-dependence. Our nationalism blinds us to the legitimate needs of the peoples of the world. We are tempted out of false pride to police the entire world unilaterally. We think of technology as the solution of all our human problems. Our security cannot be based on a self-centered materialism that deafens us to the cries of others as we exploit powerless people and the limited resources of this fragile planet. (Pastoral Message of the Christian Leaders of Iowa, page 6)

3. Liturgy. In accordance with the Catholic bishops' plea, Sister Mary Evelyn calls for prayer and penance, a deepened understanding of the mystery of peace expressed in the Eucharist. She reminds us all that in our pastoral letter we bishops call upon our people to join us in doing penance on Friday by eating less food and by abstaining from meat. The great challenge is to take our prayer life and live it in the midst of our world. It is so easy to compartmentalize our lives. Our culture pulls us one way; our faith compels us to another. Ultimately, we must achieve an interior renewal, a change of heart, a conversion to Christ.

4. A call to action. This book is filled with ideas for action. For too long we Catholics have lived in a world in which we were "fortress." Since 1960, with the help of Pope John XXIII and President John F. Kennedy, we have become "lighthouse." We are now in midstream America. Our voice is being heard. Twenty-five years ago it would have been unbelievable that the Catholic bishops would issue a document on peace and would be preparing a document on eco-nomics. The call for action is to our people. Power resides in their voice. We exercise leadership by being facilitators and enablers and motivators of our people. We will succeed or we will fail insofar as we begin or do not begin to act. Sister Mary Evelyn is striking the proper note. In this book she helps us to respond to that call for action.

Sister Mary Evelyn is following the leadership of that great hero of my life, Pope John XXIII. She is, in the tradition of his encyclical *Peace on Earth (Pacem in Terris),* recognizing that people are living "in constant fear of nuclear weapons." Monsignor Luigi G. Ligutti, who died just a year ago, called this the greatest encyclical ever written. This book can help each of us be that person described in *Pacem in Terris:* "Every believer in this world of ours must be a spark of light, a center of love, a vivifying leaven. . . . " Pope John XXIII in 1963 called our task "immense":

"There is an immense task incumbent on all men (and women) of good will, namely, the task of restoring the relations of the human family in truth, in justice, in love and in freedom. . . . "

Most Reverend Maurice J. Dingman
Bishop of Des Moines

January 1985

Introduction
The Politics of Love at Work

During the summer between my junior and senior years of high school, when I was working for my father in the family florist shop, the United States dropped the atomic bombs on Hiroshima and Nagasaki. My father said simply that the war would soon be over. He was correct. A few days later we closed early, went to the cathedral to say a prayer, and stopped at the Tribune Tower to buy a special issue of the *Chicago Tribune,* which my father said would be a historic issue.

Yet, the war that hardly broke the routine of a teenager in Chicago was, as anthropologist Margaret Mead noted, the dividing line not between two generations but between two civilizations. What happened in World War II radically changed the inner universe of our consciousness, of our sensibilities, of our moral powers — even though there is now an entire generation that cannot remember Hiroshima. We are in a state of shock, numbed by an event beyond our imagination and somehow still beyond our compassion. We are sick, and we do not know it. Can we be cured?

Hiroshima brought to a climax a way of relating to people not as members of the same human family but as enemies to be brought to unconditional surrender by a total victory. The psychology of total victory, of unconditional surrender, antedates the Bomb, of course, but use of the Bomb "to bring an end to the war" translated the attitude into an act of a new kind. The political-military establishment has told us we must be willing and able to kill children in their classrooms, old people in their beds, mothers and fathers in their homes and at work, to defend our way of life, our honor.

In placing such a high priority on defense through nuclear deterrence we have forced millions of our people to turn their vital energies, day in, day out, year in, year out, to the manufacture of life-destroying rather than life-enhancing "goods," and those people have had to pay a penalty. Whether we turn out a painting that hangs in the Metropolitan Museum or a freshly painted room, whether we make a Supreme Court decision or an apple pie, whether we design a nuclear-powered missile or one of its components, what we make becomes an extension of ourselves. In making something we are at the same time making ourselves, changing ourselves, growing or diminishing. All life-enhancing works can, and do, bring us into communion: such works as a meal, a song, a parade, the telephone, a good piece of legislation. Life-destroying works drive us apart through the fear, suspicion, and anxiety they create: such works as slings, arrows, swords, spears, guns, bombs, missiles.

We are now at a hinge of history. A persistent, rugged, common sense tells us that our way of life, our honor, cannot survive another holocaust. For as Father Dick McSorley, S.J., has cautioned, although Soviet weapons can destroy our bodies, our willingness to use nuclear weapons can destroy our souls. Our survival depends on our cure, on whether we are given the insight to see that defense could be better provided by tools and works of communion than by the tools and works of alienation. Our salvation depends on our obedience to God's command to keep the Sabbath holy, to take time out to contemplate the works of our hands, to pay attention to what we have done, to take care, to be full of care, lest we destroy the fragile ecosystem that we call home. If we want to keep the planet for the family, we will have to treat it, and one another, with much greater gentleness and respect.

I find great hope in the young who are claiming their dignity by asserting their right to refuse to kill, and I find enormous comfort in the fact that the Church is supporting these conscientious objectors — certainly by an increasingly clear and developed pastoral theology, and less evenly by adequate pastoral counseling and support. The genius of love at work springs from such a recognition of human

14

dignity, of each person as infinitely precious, with a meaning immeasurable by any of the norms we use for assessing the worth or value of economic goods.

Yesterday, coming home on a crowded airline flight, my attention was captured by a young mother and her baby boy. How fragile, how absolutely dependent for survival he was, and how marvelous. Studying him, thinking about his promise and his hope for the future, I could not escape the fact that God became just like him. As always, I was uncomfortable with the thought, as I am uncomfortable with all the other truths of my faith that hang on this central mystery of God's love saving us from inside our own flesh and bone, nerve and muscle, mind and heart.

How can I comprehend such grace? Yet, if we are to be saved from the consequences of permitting the nuclear competition that is driving us to destruction, it will be as a consequence of grace, the gift to accept ourselves as we truly are: fragile, weak, disordered — yet loved and loving, a little less than the angels, entrusted with each other's lives. How delicate is the balance on which our survival depends!

Perhaps we are at last coming to see that our most deadly enemy is fear. We are frightened almost to death by our ingenious hostility, which has wired the earth for genocide. We cannot conquer that enemy; we can only be delivered from it by love in the form of trust. Gandhi knew that the only safe way to overcome an enemy is to make of the enemy a friend. Are we capable of receiving the gift on which our cure depends? We are schooled to believe that we cannot trust the Soviets, and yet, if we are honest, we admit that we cannot even trust ourselves.

Only you, Lord, can save us from ourselves. It is not the technology that threatens us. It is not the Soviet Union. It is the killer in our own hearts, in the hearts of Christians, in *my* heart, which stands in the way of your Spirit filling the earth, making it safe and nurturing.

Save us from ourselves, Lord. Stay with us while you tutor us in the politics of love.

Part One

The Teaching
of Jesus
and the Church

CHAPTER 1

The Teaching of Jesus on Love and Nonviolence

Handling Everyday Conflict

Conflict is as much a part of life as eating and just as natural. One of the costliest mistakes we can make is to try to eliminate conflict from our lives. We do much better when we try, realistically, not to eliminate conflict but to manage it. Let me illustrate.

John, age 18, and his dad both want the family's only car at the same time. This is a simple conflict of interests. We can imagine a whole range of responses by each of them. If, a year later, John and his dad have a deeper, more mature relationship, it will be thanks to the way they managed this and many other conflicts that are part and parcel of their lives. They will have learned by practice that they had conflicting claims to a limited object, and that they found a good way to manage their conflicts. What is that way? Basically, it is the art of calling on the deepest powers they possess: mutual esteem and a willingness to give a little. Looked at another way, they tried love, and it worked.

Years before the conflict over the car, John had to learn to share toys, to lose as well as win in sports, to give some time to family chores as well as to his own interests. These were all conflict situations, and he learned to settle them all nonviolently. His father, too, learned to handle conflicts well. He had innumerable daily opportunities to practice in his work. Occasionally there was a major conflict: the promotion of one person rather than another; the chance to make a deal at the price of integrity.

Private, Social, International Conflicts

We often experience conflict even when there is no one else in sight. Should I enjoy this food or keep my weight down? Should I read this book or get a good night's sleep? Should I change jobs or settle for my present situation? In each of these conflicts it is genuine love for my "better self" as well as love for another that makes possible a nonviolent solution.

In any social situation it takes two to make a conflict and, also, two sides to make peace. Except in the case of international conflicts, we have long ruled out the use of violence in peacemaking. The pitcher may not apply his fist to the umpire; the mayor may not throw his gavel at the obstructionist city council member; and husbands and wives may not settle their conflicts by throwing the furniture at each other.

When governments of nations are in serious conflict, however, each side mobilizes its citizens. It trains them to maximum violence against the soldiers of the conflicting nation, as well as against any civilians who happen to be in the way. This is accepted by most people as legal and by many as moral. Ordinarily, it is presented by the leaders of any nation as a sacred duty of defense.

An Entirely New Situation

Today we are in a new situation in human world history. For the first time the legalized violence of war can no longer be counted on to protect those things we must be willing to defend even with our lives. This realization has been around for some time, but has not yet affected the way governments plan and prepare to defend their countries. Acutely aware of some of the implications of modern weaponry, the Second Vatican Council called for an "entirely new attitude" toward war. Our own U.S. bishops, in their 1983 pastoral letter, *The Challenge of Peace: God's Promise and Our Response,* say that "the point has been reached where public opinion sees clearly that, with the massive weaponry of the present, war is no longer viable." Pope John Paul II wrote in 1982:

> ... *the nuclear terror that haunts our time can encourage us to enrich our common heritage with a very simple discovery that is within our reach, namely that war is the most barbarous and least effective way of resolving conflicts. More than ever before, human society is forced to provide itself with the means of consultation and dialogue which it needs in order to survive, and therefore with the institutions necessary for building up justice and peace.* (World Day of Peace Message, 1982: "Peace: A Gift of God Entrusted to Us")

War: An Unnecessary Evil

The legalized violence of war, whatever good may have been preserved by it, has been at a terrible human cost. The enormity of human destruction and suffering should itself cause us to reject any notion that war is inevitable, a kind of necessary evil. Rather, war is an unnecessary evil. To succumb to a widespread and stubborn myth that we must have wars tells us something about the way we view God and our own human freedom. For many thousands of years people thought slavery was inevitable, but we would not claim that today. We abolished slavery when we came to recognize it as morally intolerable, and we will abolish war for the same reason.

What our present situation is bringing home to us at last is the deep human diminishment caused by giving in to the ways of war. Now that government leaders in the United States talk about the killing of twenty million persons as an acceptable loss in "winning" a war, the moral horror of war is coming home to us in a new way. We ask ourselves about the spiritual and moral state of an individual or nation willing to perpetrate such an atrocity. Whatever war may have been like in the days of knights and armor, today it involves indiscriminate killing on a massive scale. We cannot condone such action by any nation. Today war and the preparation for war are destroying the energies of creative love and brutalizing entire nations, blocs, and cultures.

The Way of Jesus

Like us, Jesus had to handle personal and social conflicts all his life. He experienced political conflict, too, as one who lived under Roman occupation. How did he handle conflict? As followers of Jesus, what can we learn from him about managing those conflicts that are part of the very fabric of our lives?

One of the striking features of Jesus' approach to conflict, as to almost everything, is a certain freshness and originality — a genuine creativity. Jesus' starting point for facing any life situation was his experience of God. He called God by a most unconventional name, *Abba*, which is a familiar way of saying "Father." We are accustomed to calling God "Our Father" because we have been taught to do so by Jesus. When he called God "Father" or "Abba" he brought to his people, and to us, a new way of experiencing God. He was claiming the most intimate relationship of a child to a dearly loved and most familiar parent. The term expressed even more than affectionate intimacy; it conveyed something of the nature of physical relationship. After all, the only thing that makes one a father is to beget a child.

Grounded in a radical trust in his God whom he knew as "Abba," Jesus was a trusting, unthreatened person. Power went out from him, the power of being in the truth, of experiencing true relationship with God, with others, and with all of creation. Jesus radiated an inner security and freedom of spirit. He was not threatened by conflict, and so he was able to treat his opponents with reverence, courage, and generous love.

Jesus had a strong desire to share his experience of being grounded in the unfailing, steadfast love of Our Father. This shines through all the Gospel accounts, in his words and in his response to conflict when it touched his own life, especially when it was a matter of life and death. In the Gospel of Luke he tells us:

> *But you, you must not set your hearts on things to eat and things to drink; nor must you worry. It is the pagans of this world who set their hearts on all these things. Your Father well knows you need them. No; set your hearts on his kingdom, and these other things will be given you as well.* (Luke 12:29-31)

> *And going on a little further he fell on his face and prayed. "My Father," he said, "if it is possible, let this cup pass me by. Nevertheless, let it be as you, not I, would have it."* (Matthew 26:39)

The Life and Vision of Jesus

The way we manage conflict may well be the single most important activity in determining the quality of our own lives. So we do well to turn to the life and teaching of Jesus for guidance in this crucial matter.

One thing we notice immediately is that Jesus was not passive in the face of conflict. He did not run from his opponents. Nor did he give in to them. In fact, he actually raised the level of conflict by openly siding with the poor and oppressed against the established

---

Jesus radiated an inner security and freedom of spirit. He was not threatened by conflict, so he was able to treat his opponents with reverence, courage, and generous love.

---

authorities. As the conflict heated up, Jesus prepared to go to Jerusalem. Jesus knew his opponents would succeed in killing him. But when he told that to his disciples, they were blinded by fear. They refused to accept his analysis of the situation. The Gospel of Mark tells us:

And he began to teach them that the Son of Man was destined to suffer grievously, to be rejected by the elders and the chief priests and the scribes, and to be put to death, and after three days to rise again; and he said all this quite openly. Then, taking him aside, Peter started to remonstrate with him. But, turning and seeing his disciples, he rebuked Peter and said to him, "Get behind me, Satan! Because the way you think is not God's way but man's." (Mark 8:31-33)

All creative people are moved by some great idea. Think, for example, of Martin Luther King's "I Have a Dream" speech. Jesus, too, was motivated by a central vision that kept everything in focus and gave life its richest meaning. Jesus called his vision the "kingdom of God," that is, the fullness of God's work of love in creation. Jesus' vocation was to labor for the coming of this kingdom. To be faithful to his vocation he gathered disciples to share in his mission. In the Gospel of Luke he announces:

The spirit of the Lord has been given to me,
for he has anointed me.
He has sent me to bring the good news to the poor,
to proclaim liberty to captives
and to the blind new sight,
to set the downtrodden free,
to proclaim the Lord's year of favour. (Luke 4:18-19)

Later on, the same Gospel records the following:

*After this the Lord appointed seventy-two others and
sent them out ahead of him, in pairs, to all the towns
and places he himself was to visit. He said to them, "The
harvest is rich but the labourers are few, so ask the Lord
of the harvest to send labourers to his harvest."* (Luke
10:1-2)

Disciples of Jesus

When we stop to think about it, recognizing ourselves as disciples
of Jesus puts everything in our lives into focus. It gives us a measuring
stick for making decisions about what we will or will not do. We
need to realize that Jesus, too, was a disciple. A disciple is one who
learns through association with a master teacher, learns by sharing in
the teacher's life as well as listening to his words. Jesus was a disciple
of Our Father, and his deepest longing for his own disciples was to
bring them into the communion he enjoyed with the God he trusted
and in whose love he rejoiced. The Gospel of John reflects this
longing:

*I pray not only for these,
but for those also
who through their words will believe in me.
May they all be one.
Father, may they be one in us,
as you are in me and I am in you,
so that the world may believe it was you who sent me.*
(John 17:20-21)

**A disciple is one who learns through association
with a master teacher, learns by sharing in the
teacher's life as well as by listening to his words.**

Because of his faithfulness, Jesus was able to give us his peace, the peace that the world cannot give (John 14:27). By laying down his life for us, his friends, Jesus forever transformed human life, redeeming it from death and hopelessness. In his Resurrection we share in his eternal life.

Our life achieves the meaning God intends for it to the extent that we are disciples of Jesus. The prayer that wells up from our hearts is one that welled up from the heart of Jesus: *" . . . Each morning he wakes me to hear, to listen like a disciple. The Lord Yahweh has opened my ear."* (Isaiah 50:4) We now want to look carefully at the way of discipleship in our conflict-ridden world that is threatened by violence unlike anything known before.

Free to Love Others

First, we notice that Jesus traveled lightly and was extraordinarily attentive not only to each person he met but to all of creation. His deliberate lack of possessions and attentiveness to others are connected. Not preoccupied with "making it" for himself, Jesus was able to turn his talents and energies to the good of others. This is authentic love. Whether or not this came easily to Jesus, he knew it was not easy for his disciples. He spoke very directly to them about finding their security elsewhere than in possessions. He taught them to trust Our Father to give them what they needed each day. He saw possessions as a hazard. Note the important distinction: the world and all that is in it was good, very good in the eyes of Jesus; it was the turning of any of it into a private treasure that was self-destructive. Recall Jesus' story about the man who built bigger barns to store his ever-increasing grain:

> *But God said to him, "Fool! This very night the demand will be made for your soul; and this hoard of yours, whose will it be then?" So it is when a man stores up treasure for himself in place of making himself rich in the sight of God.* (Luke 12:20-21)

Love Without Limits

Jesus learned from his intimate relationship with Our Father that God's love is unconditional. God does not love because we are good but because he is. Jesus pointed out that Our Father lets his sun shine and rain fall on good and bad alike (Matthew 5:43-48). Being Our Father's disciple, Jesus loved others not because of their merits but because of their need. What a difference this made to uncounted sick and troubled people, as we learn from even a casual reading of the Gospels. This unconditional love also made possible the reconciliation with Peter after he had denied Jesus three times. It accounts for Jesus' patience in dealing with disciples who possessed a mixture of lovable and exasperating qualities, just as we do. We find no Gospel evidence of Jesus defining persons or groups as unworthy of attention or practical love.

Not preoccupied with "making it" for himself, Jesus was able to turn his talents and energies to the good of others.

Love is eminently practical. This is at the heart of Jesus' teaching. In a story which expresses his central moral teaching, Jesus does not use the word *love*; rather, he describes it in action:

> ... *Come, you whom my Father has blessed, take for your heritage the kingdom prepared for you since the foundation of the world. For I was hungry and you gave me food; I was thirsty and you gave me drink.* ...
> (Matthew 25:34,35)

Other parables, such as The Prodigal Son and The Good Samaritan, are about unconditional love responding to need. These ways of love — feeding the hungry, giving drink to the thirsty, clothing the naked, sheltering the homeless, caring for the sick, visiting those in prison — are works of mercy and, therefore, works of peace. It is sobering to realize that wars not only put a halt to works of mercy and peace but actually reverse them by causing hunger, starvation, famine, polluted water supplies, destroyed homes, overcrowded prison camps, and even desecrated burial places.

Love of Enemies

Jesus was aware that his teaching contained ideas that would be stumbling blocks to many. But that did not lead him to water down his teaching. He concentrated his efforts on forming true disciples.

Being our Father's disciple, Jesus loved others not because of their merits but because of their need.

One of the stumbling blocks in his teaching is that we are to love our enemies. For Jesus, love is proved in action. So love of enemies means much more than refusal to harm them. It means being careful to do good to them, to see that they have food, clothing, shelter, support — in short, all the things they need. It means:

> *... Love your enemies, do good to those who hate you, bless those who curse you, pray for those who treat you badly.* (Luke 6:27,28)

This may strike us as preposterous or, at least, as impractical advice — especially if we replace the general term *enemy* with some specific person or group, such as the Soviet Union or Cuba or persons we have lost contact with because of deep hurts ages ago.

For Jesus, the result of refusing to love our enemies is terrifying. We cannot have a good relationship with God unless we attempt reconciliation. He says:

> *Be compassionate as your Father is compassionate. Do not judge, and you will not be judged yourselves; do not condemn, and you will not be condemned yourselves; grant pardon, and you will be pardoned. Give, and there will be gifts for you: a full measure, pressed down, shaken together, and running over, will be poured into your lap; because the amount you measure out is the amount you will be given back.* (Luke 6:36-38)

The violence of war has been legalized for fifteen hundred years. So, as a matter of course, many people even today see war as normal and necessary. Consequently, the teaching of Jesus about resolving conflicts through love of enemies can seem strange and impractical. And yet, the lesson of history is that a little violence leads to more and more. We have gone from the wooden club to the intercontinental ballistic missile, and all in the name of defense of those we love. Many men, we must remember, have nobly given their lives in the effort to make peace through war. We have learned a way of moral argument that has enabled us to establish conditions for killing our enemies so long as they are combatants and we ourselves are in a defensive war, a war which fulfills several other conditions of the "just war theory." Without coming to any conclusion here about the value and usefulness of that theory, we still need to ponder the meaning and application of Jesus' teaching about love of enemies. What would happen if NATO came up with a plan to help the USSR in commercial shipping through easier access to warmwater ports? Or if the USA and Cuba developed a joint plan for promoting literacy training in Central America? Or if you or I took some creative initiative toward someone we hurt months or years ago, which left both sides with psychological and emotional scars or even with open wounds? These things are terribly risky, we think, and we add that it is better to play it safe, to keep conditions as they are. But for us, the persistent question remains, Is this the way of Jesus?

The teaching of Jesus about resolving conflicts through love of enemies can seem strange and impractical. And yet, the lesson of history is that a little violence leads to more and more.

Love of enemies is costly. This, too, we learn from the life of Jesus. He could have avoided his death had he simply withdrawn from the struggle. Or he could have organized an armed opposition to the corrupt leaders of his own people who were collaborating with the oppressor. He could have joined a movement to throw off the Roman yoke or, at least, a movement that involved violence to bring about relief from Roman oppression. Jesus' way was not any of these — but neither was it passivity in the face of opposition. His way of response was to act out the truth in love. He showed us that the most powerful, profoundly creative way to overcome enemies is to make them our friends. This he did by being faithful to the struggle for justice and truth, even to death. Jesus taught us how to live and how to die. He gave us no guidance on how to kill in a good cause. As the U.S. Catholic bishops explain in their pastoral letter, *The Challenge of Peace:*

> *Most characteristic of Jesus' actions are those in which he showed his love. As he had commanded others, his love led him even to the giving of his own life to effect redemption. Jesus' message and his actions were dangerous ones in his time, and they led to his death — a cruel and viciously inflicted death, a criminal's death (Gal. 3:13). In all of his suffering, as in all of his life and*

30

ministry, Jesus refused to defend himself with force or with violence. He endured violence and cruelty so that God's love might be fully manifest and the world might be reconciled to the One from whom it had become estranged. Even at his death, Jesus cried out for forgiveness for those who were his executioners: "Father, forgive them" (Lk. 23:34).

The resurrection of Jesus is the sign to the world that God indeed does reign, does give life in death and that the love of God is stronger even than death (Rom. 8:36-39). (The Challenge of Peace, 49-50)

Our Way of Life

We know from Jesus not only the cost of discipleship but also its consequences. Jesus' Resurrection is the ultimate vindication of his way of nonviolence, of doing the truth in love. In Jesus we know the highest possibility for human life. The way of Jesus brings God into a concrete situation in a redeeming way. Jesus himself is our way, our truth, and our life (John 14:6).

We have a stake in conflict resolution on all levels — in our personal lives, in our communities, and in our world where millions are victims of the violence of injustice. Today all of us face the threat of annihilation through the technology we have developed for the sake of security. What can we learn from reflecting on the way of Gospel nonviolence, the way of Jesus?

First, the way of Jesus is a way of struggle. It involves pain, but pain borne by ourselves. It refuses to achieve its goal by destroying others. For disciples of Jesus, this means the effort to cooperate rather than compete, to do good to all rather than to win out over our adversaries. It means experimenting with the power of love and truth in concrete situations.

Second, the way of Gospel nonviolence puts the Works of Mercy into the center of our lives. We make major career decisions as well as many daily decisions on the basis of the good we can do to our brothers and sisters regardless of where they live, what they believe, or what they can do to us.

He showed us that the most powerful, profoundly creative way to overcome enemies is to make them our friends.

Third, we find ourselves asking questions about policies of national defense when they do not express love of enemies, for we know that love must find its proper political expression. We resist any attempt to protect human rights for ourselves by causing or tolerating hunger, thirst, starvation, famine, homelessness for anyone else. We are among the growing number of persons around the globe who openly say that war is obsolete, that we are now called to trust Our Father and reclaim our dignity, our ability to talk our way to peace rather than kill our way to mutual destruction.

Fourth, we need to offer and receive support from others in our effort to learn Gospel nonviolence, the way of Jesus. The pastoral letter of the American bishops, *The Challenge of Peace,* tells us:

> *We readily recognize that we live in a world that is becoming increasingly estranged from Christian values. In order to remain a Christian, one must take a resolute stand against many commonly accepted axioms of the world. To become true disciples, we must undergo a demanding course of induction into the adult Christian community. We must continually equip ourselves to profess the full faith of the church in an increasingly secularized society. We must develop a sense of solidarity, cemented by relationships with ma-*

*ture and exemplary Christians who represent Christ
and his way of life.*

*All of these comments about the meaning of being a
disciple or a follower of Jesus today are especially
relevant to the quest for genuine peace in our time.* (*The
Challenge of Peace,* 277-278)

Points for Discussion

1. List a half dozen or more conflicts that most families usually settle peacefully. Focus on how each of these conflicts is usually resolved. Identify any common thread(s) running through these peaceful resolutions.

2. Vatican II and the U.S. Catholic bishops call for an "entirely new attitude" toward war. From your own knowledge, list basic features of the old attitude. List reasons given in this chapter why a new attitude is needed. Alongside the old, list basic features of a new attitude based on a Christian outlook.

3. How did Jesus handle the conflicts in his own life? Give examples from this chapter and from the New Testament.

4. What does it mean to be a disciple? What basic characteristics can we expect to see in the life-style of a disciple of Jesus?

5. List some practical consequences (a) in family life, (b) in international relations, of taking seriously Jesus' teaching to love our enemies. Discuss the hidden (a) psychological and (b) religious assumptions behind the idea that this teaching is not practical.

6. Discuss each of the four consequences of Christian discipleship given at the end of this chapter. List ways we can make them part of our lives.

Recommended Reading

Christ and Violence by Ronald Sider. Herald Press, 1979. Paperback. A challenge to Christians about the relevance of Jesus for issues of justice and peace.

Facing Nuclear War by Donald B. Kraybill. Herald Press, 1982. Paperback. Blends biblical and political reasons for abandoning the arms race. Simple, excellent study guide for youth and adult study groups.

Peacemakers: Christian Voices from the New Abolitionist Movement. Jim Wallis, Editor. Harper & Row, 1983. Paperback. Powerful testimony by Christian leaders telling why nuclear weapons are unacceptable. One of the articles in *Peacemakers* became the Introduction to the book you are now reading.

Waging Peace: A Handbook for the Struggle to Abolish Nuclear Weapons. Edited by Jim Wallis. Harper & Row, 1982. Paperback. A handbook for those who want to become informed and involved. Excellent resource for small groups, CCD, etc. (Large quantity discounts available from Sojourners Book Service, P.O. Box 29272, Washington, D.C. 20017.)

CHAPTER 2

The Peace Doctrine
of Pope John Paul II

Those of us who live in Chicago will never forget the Pope's visit in October 1979. The city was alive with excitement. Chicago has the second largest community of Polish people in the world. Yet, for a couple of days this city of many cultures became one big happy family, welcoming one of our own. People who ordinarily shun crowds waited for hours on street corners simply to wave at the Pope. Young people gathered outside his window at night for a singalong. For hours before the outdoor Mass in Grant Park all traffic seemed to be moving in only one direction.

We would have gathered to greet the Pope in any case. But we recognized that Pope John Paul II radiates a very special sense of hope and faith in people, a genuine love that shows itself in spontaneous affection.

These same characteristics mark John Paul II's many writings on peace. He is pointing humankind out of the century marked by the bloodiest wars in history, through the dark and terrifying tunnel of the arms race threatening us with absolute ruin. He is pointing us into a new era where we can claim our dignity as human persons who manage our conflicts by dialogue and negotiation rather than by war.

In that prophetic vein, this chapter looks at the first four years of Pope John Paul's peacemaking efforts. It records how he is helping us to undertake the *"evaluation of war with an entirely new attitude"* called for by the Second Vatican Council (Church in the Modern World, 80).

Our New Consciousness

Today a new truth about peace is dawning on human consciousness. As surely as we recognize a sunrise, more and more people are coming to the realization that a nuclear war would have no winners. It would very likely extinguish civilization. Peace is an absolute necessity as it has never been before. Will the human family act on this new understanding of war and peace? If we do, history will recognize that one of the persons who did most to educate us about our new moment in history is Pope John Paul II.

Pope John Paul has traveled to all parts of the world, teaching about our call to peacemaking. The Pope has been deeply moved by the terrible violence of our time and has come to grips with its meaning. Some of his most moving words have been on the very sites of the greatest suffering.

A case in point is his visit to Japan in February 1981. In Hiroshima's Memorial Peace Park, Pope John Paul explained that he wanted to make the visit to Hiroshima *"out of a deep personal conviction that to remember the past is to commit oneself to the future."* Commitment to the future of the human family threatened with complete destruction is at the heart of all the Pope's tireless efforts for peace. His is a profound vision of the beauty and possibility of the human person. History, the Pope is convinced, now presents humankind with the responsibility to live in peace. We can do this by making a collective option to solve conflicts by dialogue and negotiation rather than by the organized violence of war.

To a group of scholars and scientists at the United Nations University in Hiroshima the Pope said:

> *Surely the time has come for our society and especially for the world of science to realize that the future of humanity depends as never before on our collective moral choices.*
>
> *In the past, it was possible to destroy a village, a town, a region, even a country. Now it is the whole*

planet that has come under threat. This fact should finally compel everyone to face a basic moral consideration: from now on, it is only through a conscious choice and through a deliberate policy that humanity can survive. . . .

Our future on this planet, exposed as it is to nuclear annihilation, depends upon one single factor: humanity must make a moral about-face.

Seven Principles for Survival

Within a few months after his election late in 1978, Pope John Paul delivered his first major peace message — on January 1, 1979, the World Day of Peace. The message was entitled, "To Reach Peace, Teach Peace." Seen from today's perspective, we can recognize in that first message several characteristics that mark the Pope's later peace efforts. Noting as a positive sign the growing public opinion that would no longer tolerate war, he sees in this a challenge to take up the long and difficult task of moving beyond slogans. He outlines seven principles in which people must trust as the basis for peace.

"Our future on this planet, exposed as it is to nuclear annihilation, depends upon one single factor: humanity must make a moral about-face." — **Pope John Paul II**

An examination of these principles makes clear how forthright and concrete the Pope's teaching is. His later words on many occasions have underscored the fact that these principles are not mere wishes but genuine "rules of the game" by which the human family must abide if we are to have a future. The seven principles, in the Pope's own words, are:

1. *Human affairs must be dealt with humanely, not with violence.*

2. *Tensions, rivalries and conflicts must be settled by reasonable negotiations and not by force.*

3. *Opposing ideologies must confront each other in a climate of dialogue and free discussion.*

4. *The legitimate interests of particular groups must also take into account the legitimate interests of the other groups involved and of the demands of the higher common good.*

5. *Recourse to arms cannot be considered the right means for settling conflicts.*

6. *The inalienable human rights must be safeguarded in every circumstance.*

7. *It is not permissible to kill in order to impose a solution.*

Violence Is a Lie

Pope John Paul rejects all notions that violence is inevitable or normal for humanity. In his view, violence itself is a lie in the sense that it goes against the deepest power of the human heart, which is the power of love and reconciliation.

Several times since January 1979, the Pope has developed this idea. On his trip to Ireland in September 1979, he spoke to an enormous gathering at Drogheda, near the border of Northern Ireland. There he declared:

> *Violence is a lie, for it goes against the truth of our faith, the truth of our humanity. Violence destroys what it claims to defend: the dignity, the life, the freedom of human beings. Violence is a crime against humanity, for it destroys the very fabric of society. . . . To all of you*

who are listening I say: Do not believe in violence; do not support violence. It is not the Christian way. It is not the way of the Catholic Church. Believe in peace and forgiveness and love; for they are of Christ.

The notion of violence as a lie is an idea that Pope John Paul developed further in the 1980 World Day of Peace message, "Truth, the Power of Peace." In that message he explains:

Violence flourishes in lies, and needs lies. . . . What should one say of the practice of combatting or silencing those who do not share the same views by labelling them as enemies, attributing to them hostile intentions and using skillful and constant propaganda to brand them as aggressors?

He holds that "the first lie," "the basic falsehood," is to refuse to believe in the human person, who has a capacity for greatness and a need to be redeemed from evil and sin within.

Violence Never Brings Peace

Pope John Paul adamantly rejects the notion that violence produces peace or that humanity achieves progress principally through violence. Fatalism about violence has terrible consequences.

"To all of you who are listening I say: Do not believe in violence; do not support violence. It is not the Christian way. It is not the way of the Catholic Church. Believe in peace and forgiveness and love; for they are of Christ."
— **Pope John Paul II**

One can think of the arms race, and also of guerrilla warfare, in connection with the following:

> *Of course, this widespread tendency to have recourse to trials of strength in order to make justice is often held in check by tactical or strategic pauses. But, as long as threats are permitted to remain, as long as selective support is given to certain forms of violence in line with interests or ideologies, as long as support is given to the claim that the advance of justice comes, in the final analysis, through violent struggle — as long as these things happen, then niceties, restraint and selectivity will periodically give way in the face of the simple and brutal logic of violence, a logic which can go as far as the suicidal exaltation of violence for its own sake.*
> ("Truth, the Power of Peace," 1980)

Peace Comes Through Negotiating

The Pope has labored to bring home to others what he sees so clearly: that people usually solve conflicts reasonably on the personal level and that we can also use our negotiating and reconciling abilities to solve conflicts within and among nations. The alternative today would be so horrible that we cannot imagine it. Pope John Paul sent a commission of scientists to the heads of the states possessing nuclear weapons to make clear to them that scientific expertise has no way to provide recovery and healing in the event of a nuclear catastrophe.

The Pope's adherence to the principle that conflicts must be settled by negotiation and not by force seems to spring in part from his acute sense of the enormous injustice of handing on to the young a runaway arms race that is leading to destruction. When he spoke to the General Assembly of the United Nations in October 1979, he closed his address with reflections on responsibility for children. He said:

> *Concern for the child ... even before birth, from the first moment of conception and then throughout the years of infancy and youth, is the primary and fundamental test of the relationship of one human being to another. ... But in this perspective we must ask ourselves whether there will continue to accumulate over the heads of this new generation of children the threat of common extermination for which the means are in the hands of the modern states, especially the major world powers. Are the children to receive the arms race from us as a necessary inheritance? How are we to explain this unbridled race?*

The Need for Dialogue

The need and possibility of dialogue is a principal theme of the Pope's teaching on peace. In the 1982 World Day of Peace message, "Peace: A Gift of God Entrusted to Us," Pope John Paul addresses the problem of harmonizing the right and duty of defense with the need to reject unjust means. The Pope finds dialogue a way out of the dilemma:

"Concern for the child ... is the primary and fundamental test of the relationship of one human being to another. ... Are the children to receive the arms race from us as a necessary inheritance? How are we to explain this unbridled race?" — **Pope John Paul II**

Christians, even as they strive to resist and prevent every form of warfare, have no hesitation in recalling that in the name of an elementary requirement of justice, peoples have a right and even a duty to protect their existence and freedom by proportionate means against an unjust aggressor.

However, in view of the difference between classical warfare and nuclear or bacteriological war — a difference so to speak of nature — and in view of the scandal of the arms race seen against the background of the needs of the Third World, this right, which is very real in principle, only underlines the urgency for world society to equip itself with effective means of negotiation.

In this way the nuclear terror that haunts our time can encourage us to enrich our common heritage with a very simple discovery that is within our reach, namely, that war is the most barbarous and least effective way of resolving conflicts. More than ever before, human society is forced to provide itself with the means of consultation and dialogue which it needs in order to survive, and therefore with the institutions necessary for building up justice and peace.

The Pope highlighted dialogue in an address he sent to the United Nations Second Special Session on Disarmament in 1982, and he also made it the theme of his World Day of Peace message in 1983. This message, "Dialogue: The Peacemaker's Task," is a masterful treatise not only on the need for dialogue but also on obstacles to it and ways of fostering it. The Pope, who knows communist rule firsthand, insists on approaching adversaries with openness and trust in the ability to come to agreement. Dialogue, he says,

is a wager on the social nature of people, on their calling to go forward together, with continuity — by a

converging meeting of minds, wills, hearts — toward
the goal that the creator has fixed for them. The goal is
to make the world a place for everybody to live in and
worthy of everybody.

Even where there are strong ideological differences, he says,

the attempt to have a lucid dialogue still seems neces-
sary in order to unblock the situation and to work for
the possible establishment of peace on particular
points. This is to be done by counting upon common
sense, on the possibilities of danger for everyone and on
the just aspirations to which peoples themselves largely
adhere.

Dialogue and Economic Justice

We have all seen the Pope on television, and know how he radiates
a sense of love and hope. He is clearly a person who sees a glass half
full where others may see it half empty. On the one hand, he has a
sense of the growing danger of a nuclear holocaust; on the other side,
this very awareness — measured against his experience of and faith
in the goodness of God and of people — impels him to keep
searching for the words, images, and ideas that will make all people
of good will invest their very lives in ways of building a peaceful
world.

"War is the most barbarous and least effective
way of resolving conflicts." — Pope John Paul II

Dialogue is not to be confined only to efforts for disarmament,
crucial as that is. Rather, dialogue must extend to all the areas that
threaten the good of persons and their communities. The most

fundamental threat is the structured violence of injustice. He explains:

> *Dialogue for peace will also necessarily involve a discussion of the rules which govern economic life. For the temptation to violence and war will always be present in societies where greed and the search for material goods impels a wealthy minority to refuse the mass of people the satisfaction of the most elementary rights to food, education, health and life.*

Truth and the Human Spirit

We are tempted to think that "anything goes" in a struggle against atheistic communism. Pope John Paul urges us, time and time again, to distinguish between people and ideology. His own position is, clearly, that we do not overcome ideological differences by destroying people but by carefully fostering truth wherever it is found. Part of the truth is that our opponents have some legitimate claims and interests. We need to be sensitive to these legitimate claims and honor them. This is the only way to achieve an environment which fosters total human development for each person and for all together.

This common good is much more than material growth; it also means the opportunity to satisfy the deepest spiritual longings expressed in worship, culture, and the arts. A few examples of Pope John Paul's words will illustrate this important dimension. In his address to the United Nations in 1979, he said:

> *Permit me, distinguished ladies and gentlemen, to recall a constant rule of the history of humanity, a rule that is implicitly contained in all that I have already stated with regard to integral development and human*

rights. The rule is based on the relationship between spiritual values and material or economic values. In this relationship, it is the spiritual values that are pre-eminent, both on account of the nature of these values and also for reasons concerning the good of the person. The pre-eminence of the values of the spirit defines the proper sense of earthly material goods and the way to use them. . . . Indeed, the more people share in such goods, the more they are enjoyed and drawn upon, the more then do those goods show their indestructible and immortal worth. This truth is confirmed, for example, by the works of creativity — I mean by the works of thought, poetry, music, and the figurative arts, fruits of the human spirit.

Rejection of War

One of the principles the Pope set down in his first World Day of Peace message is: *"Recourse to arms cannot be considered the right means for settling conflicts."* This principle will continue to be pondered as the whole Church labors to make moral judgments about modern warfare in light of the traditional just-war teaching, which has been used as a guide since the fourth century. This is not to say that the just-war theory condoned all wars, far from it. But the just-war theory does not take so categorical an approach as the principle Pope John Paul stated. The Pope has not tried to explain away his statement nor to soften it. Rather, he emphasized his position in Coventry, England, at the restored cathedral which incorporates bombed ruins — eloquent testimony to the ravages of war. He said:

Today the scale and the horror of modern warfare — whether nuclear or not — makes it totally unacceptable as a means of settling differences between nations.

In both the 1982 and 1983 World Day of Peace messages the Pope has discussed specific characteristics of modern warfare which call for a fresh appraisal of war. In 1982 he pointed to three new characteristics:

(1) Conflicts today have worldwide repercussions because of growing economic interdependence.

(2) They are total because they mobilize all the forces of the nation involved.

(3) They are radical because *"it is the survival of the whole human race that is at stake in them, given the destructive capacity of present-day military stockpiles."*

"Today the scale and the horror of modern warfare — whether nuclear or not — makes it totally unacceptable as a means of settling differences between nations."
— **Pope John Paul II**

In 1983 John Paul II spoke even more specifically about wars since 1945, pointing out that *"contrary to a widespread opinion, one can, alas, number more than 150 armed conflicts since the Second World War [because] people have shown that they preferred to use arms rather than to try to understand one another."* Of these wars, he says:

> *Now, who then would dare to make light of such wars — some of which are still going on — or of states of war, or of the deep frustrations that wars leave behind? Who would dare, without trembling, to envisage even more extensive and much more terrible wars which still threaten?*
>
> *Is it not necessary to give everything in order to avoid war, even limited war (thus euphemistically called by*

those who are not directly concerned in it), given the evil that every war represents, its price which must be paid in human lives, in suffering, in the devastation of what would be necessary for human life and development, without counting the upset of necessary tranquility, the deterioration of the social fabric, the hardening of mistrust and hatred which wars maintain toward one's neighbor?

And today when even conventional wars become so murderous, when one knows the tragic consequences that nuclear war would have, the need to stop war or to turn aside its threat is all the more imperious. And thus we see as more fundamental the need to have recourse to dialogue, to its political strength, which must avoid recourse to arms.

Human Rights, Justice, and Peace

The recognition of the intimate relationship between peace and justice is found in the Old Testament — for example, in the Prophets and the Psalms. This awareness also permeates the life and teaching of Jesus. For Pope John Paul, the link between peace and justice is in human rights, those inalienable claims to what a person and community need to live in accord with our dignity as image and child of God. The Pope has praised the work of the United Nations in the field of human rights, and he has helped create a deeper understanding of the need. He has been especially effective in making a case for religious liberty as a right which safeguards the deepest dimensions of the person, and he also has spoken very bluntly of the contradiction between the profession of respect for human rights and the practice which denies those same rights. He points out such abuses as denial of freedom of worship and also the exploitation of poor nations for the economic advantage of the rich and powerful. Readers in both East and West, North and South, have much to examine here.

The Christian Dimension

The Pope is reaching out to all people of good will, setting forth universal principles on which many can agree. He has indomitable confidence in our ability to live worthy of the vocation to which we are called as children of a God whose love is unconditional.

Especially in his World Day of Peace messages, the Pope addresses words specifically to the Christian community. He reminds us that Jesus has reconciled us to God and to each other by his own complete gift of himself. We are to follow his way, strengthened by the gift of his Spirit. The Pope says:

> *The most faithful disciples of Christ have been builders of peace, to the point of forgiving their enemies, sometimes even to the point of giving their lives for them. Their example marks the path for a new humanity no longer content with provisional compromises but instead achieving the deepest sort of brotherhood.*
> ("To Reach Peace, Teach Peace," 1979)

A Suggestion

The teaching of Pope John Paul II on peace has received too little attention. Most Catholics and others would be both surprised and encouraged to know how the Pope is helping to develop the *"entirely new attitude"* toward war called for by the Second Vatican Council.

"The most faithful disciples of Christ have been builders of peace, to the point of forgiving their enemies, sometimes even to the point of giving their lives for them." — Pope John Paul II

You can help spread the good news by sharing this book with someone you know. You might also consider gathering a few friends for a discussion of current issues in light of the teaching found here. This could be especially helpful to those who hold responsibility for the education of the young, whether as parents, teachers, or pastors.

Points for Discussion

1. Pope John Paul II tells us that "Violence is a lie." What are the several meanings of this statement given in this chapter? Give examples.
2. Why does Pope John Paul say that peace comes through negotiating?
3. List the various points in this chapter that Pope John Paul makes regarding dialogue.
4. What does Pope John Paul say about the legitimate interests of opponents? What does he say about the higher common good?
5. What does Pope John Paul say about human rights?

The Teachings of Pope John Paul II

The most accessible printed resource in English for the teachings of Pope John Paul, including his encyclical letters, is the weekly publication *Origins,* available from National Catholic News Service, 1312 Massachusetts Avenue, Washington, D.C. 20005. Phone: 202/659-6732.

CHAPTER 3

Nuclear Weapons: Tradition and the U.S. Bishops

Danger and Opportunity

"The whole human race faces a moment of supreme crisis in its advance towards maturity." These words, from the Vatican II document The Church in the Modern World, were chosen by the bishops of the United States to open the pastoral letter on peace and war they issued on May 3, 1983.

To further emphasize the seriousness of the crisis and our inability to manage it without extraordinary help from God, the bishops have called on American Catholics to join them in their own commitment to fast and abstinence on each Friday of the year.

Clearly, the leaders of the Catholic Church in the United States recognize that we are at a new moment in world history, a moment of peril unlike anything we have ever faced before. At the same time, we are at a moment of opportunity for a historic advance toward a more human way of settling international conflicts.

Nuclear weapons are with us. Even when we dismantle them, we will still, as a human race, have the know-how for making them, and the painful memory of the atomic bombings of 1945 which set off the present arms race. This race is the great common enemy of the United States and the Soviet Union alike.

When trying to understand the moral issues of nuclear weapons, we need to consider these issues in light of what the Catholic Church teaches about war and peace. In this way we can come to a true understanding and find the hope, love, and courage to accept our share in delivering the world from the terror of nuclear weapons. We can do our part to hand on to our children a world where the enormous human effort now spent on nuclear deterrence can be redirected to promoting the human development of all the world's poor and oppressed peoples.

Catholic Teaching, Past and Present

The Church has never been silent on issues of peace and war. The roots of the Church's teaching are found in the New Testament, particularly in the Gospel accounts of the life and teachings of Jesus. We do not find there, of course, any teaching directly on the specific problems we face as the first generation to cope with nuclear weapons. The teaching which must guide us has been developed over the years, particularly since the fourth century when Christianity came out of the catacombs and was accepted by the Roman State which then ruled the known world. Since that time, Christians have been expected to give military service in defense of their countries. This poses very special problems in the nuclear age.

Our current teaching on the conditions under which Catholics may or may not morally participate in war goes back to Saint Augustine (354-430), and also draws heavily on the teaching of Saint Thomas Aquinas (1225-1274). In this chapter we are focusing on the Church's contemporary teaching, particularly as it has developed since the use of atomic weaponry at the end of World War II. We will take into consideration the teachings of three recent popes — John XXIII, Paul VI, and John Paul II — as well as the teachings of Vatican Council II (1962-1965). We will also look at the 1983 pastoral letter of the U.S. Catholic bishops, *The Challenge of Peace: God's Promise and Our Response.* This letter applies the teaching of the Church to our own situation.

Pope John XXIII

Pope John XXIII, in the encyclical letter *Peace on Earth (Pacem in Terris),* recognized that people were living in constant fear of nuclear weapons. He concluded: "Justice, right reason and humanity, therefore, urgently demand that the arms race should cease." (112)

Pope John went on to specify the demands coming from the conscience of humanity: that stockpiles of weapons should be reduced equally and simultaneously by the parties involved, and "that nuclear weapons should be banned." (112)

The Church has never been silent on issues of peace and war. The roots of the Church's teaching are found in the New Testament, particularly in the Gospel accounts of the life and teachings of Jesus.

Pope John came to this position from his reading of the signs of the times — a term he used over and over in his encyclical. One of these signs was that thoughtful people all over the world were becoming convinced that international disputes should not be resolved by recourse to arms but by negotiations. He repeated the warning of Pope Pius XII: "Nothing is lost by peace; everything may be lost by war." (112)

Pope John's principal theme in his great peace encyclical was human rights. He showed how these rights follow from our dignity as children of God, a gift shared by every member of the human race. These rights are God-given claims to all those conditions necessary to live in a way consistent with our high calling. Each right, or claim, carries a corresponding responsibility or duty. When human rights are observed, the result is peace. Peace can only be established on a foundation of justice, truth, love, and freedom. Pope John called these the four pillars of peace.

The Second Vatican Council

Two years after the encyclical *Peace on Earth,* the bishops of the entire Church, gathered in the Second Vatican Council, spoke forcefully on the question of nuclear weapons. Like Pope John, they were careful to emphasize that it is peace which must be the focus of our efforts and that this peace is both God's gift and also a human work entrusted to us. In the Pastoral Constitution on the Church in the Modern World (*Gaudium et Spes*), they assessed the new weapons of mass destruction and flatly and clearly ruled them out of bounds for use in war. In the only condemnation expressed by the entire Council they declared:

> *Any act of war aimed indiscriminately at the destruc-*
> *tion of entire cities or of extensive areas along with*
> *their population is a crime against God and man*
> *himself. It merits unequivocal and unhesitating con-*
> *demnation.* (80)

The Council Fathers recognized that many Catholics would find it a violation of conscience to become members of the armed forces, training to use nuclear weapons. This was a major factor influencing the Council's teaching on conscientious objection. The Church in the Modern World makes the stark observation:

> *Indeed, now that every kind of weapon produced by*
> *modern science is used in war, the fierce character of*
> *warfare threatens to lead the combatants to a savagery*
> *far surpassing that of the past.* (79)

The Council Fathers conclude:

> *it seems right that laws make humane provisions for the case of those who for reasons of conscience refuse to bear arms, provided however, that they accept some other form of service to the human community.* (79)

Ever since Vatican Council II, the U.S. bishops have pressed for legal recognition of both general and selective conscientious objection. *Selective* conscientious objection is based on the claim that a *specific* war violates the standards of the just-war principles that the Church has taught since the fourth century. So far this effort on the part of the Church in the United States has not been successful. In their pastoral letter the bishops once more state their support for conscientious objection, without presenting it as a universal obligation (see paragraphs 118-119). They also praise those in the military who carry out their responsibilities according to Catholic moral teaching (see paragraph 309).

"Any act of war aimed indiscriminately at the destruction of entire cities or of extensive areas along with their population is a crime against God and man himself. It merits unequivocal and unhesitating condemnation." — Vatican II

Statements from the Holy See

A careful reading of Vatican statements shows a development in the assessment that nuclear weapons are outside the bounds of moral tolerability. Both the arms race and government policies for using weapons come under increasingly strong criticism. In 1965, the Council document The Church in the Modern World called the arms race "an utterly treacherous trap for humanity" (81). In 1974, a Vatican statement called the arms race "an insanity that burdens the world." And in 1976 it was described as "a machine gone mad," driven by its own momentum. That same year, Pope Paul VI referred to the actual atomic bombing of Hiroshima and Nagasaki as "a butchery of untold magnitude."

The Church, of course, has always looked to the elimination of war as an ideal to strive for. But the massive suffering of our own century, which has seen millions killed in two world wars, and which has also seen more than ten million persons killed in sixty wars since 1965, has made the Church increasingly sensitive and supportive of those who dedicate themselves unreservedly to working for peace and the elimination of war.

While the Council was in its last session in 1965, Pope Paul VI addressed the United Nations on October 4. He praised the U.N. because it sanctions "the great principle that the relations between peoples should be regulated by reason, justice, law and negotiation; not by force, violence, war, by fear or deceit." He then spoke most solemnly those words which reflect the assessment and the longing of so many hearts.

> *It suffices to remember that the blood of millions of men, that numberless and unheard of sufferings, useless slaughter and frightful ruin, are the sanction of the past which unites you with an oath which must change the future history of the world: No more war, war never again! Peace, it is peace which must guide the destinies of peoples and of all mankind.*

The Pope also spoke of the dangers of the weapons buildup which was taking on a new significance in the nuclear age:

> *If you want to be brothers, let the weapons fall from your hands. You cannot love with weapons in your*

hands. Long before they mete out death and destruction,
those terrible arms supplied by modern science foment
bad feelings and cause nightmares, distrust, and dark
designs.

Pope John Paul II

Pope John Paul II has continued and intensified the work of his predecessors for peace. His first World Day of Peace message in 1979 established the tone of his writings and speeches which have followed in a steady stream. That message, "To Reach Peace, Teach Peace," specified the seven principles noted in the last chapter — principles which the Pope claimed could and must win universal acceptance. We repeat them here:

1. *Human affairs must be dealt with humanely, not with violence.*
2. *Tensions, rivalries and conflicts must be settled by reasonable negotiations and not by force.*
3. *Opposing ideologies must confront each other in a climate of dialogue and free discussion.*
4. *The legitimate interests of particular groups must also take into account the legitimate interests of the other groups involved and of the demands of the higher common good.*
5. *Recourse to arms cannot be considered the right means for settling conflicts.*
6. *The inalienable human rights must be safeguarded in every circumstance.*
7. *It is not permissible to kill in order to impose a solution.*

This forthright assertion that war must be ruled out as a way of resolving international disputes has been repeated on other occa-

sions by our Holy Father. Speaking in Coventry Cathedral in 1982, he
said:

> *Today, the scale and the horror of modern warfare —
> whether nuclear or not — makes it totally unac-
> ceptable as a means of settling differences between
> nations. War should belong to the tragic past, to history;
> it should find no place on humanity's agenda for the
> future.*

**Ever since Vatican Council II, our own U.S.
bishops have pressed for legal recognition of
both general and selective conscientious
objection.** *Selective* **conscientious objection is
based on the claim that a** *specific* **war violates
the standards of the just-war principles that the
Church has taught since the fourth century.**

A year earlier, standing on the site of the first atomic bombing,
Hiroshima, he said:

> *In the face of the man-made calamity that every war
> is, one must affirm and reaffirm, again and again, that
> the waging of war is not inevitable or unchangeable.
> Humanity is not destined to self-destruction. Clashes of
> ideologies, aspirations and needs can and must be
> settled and resolved by means other than war and
> violence. Humanity owes it to itself to settle differences
> and conflicts by peaceful means.*

The Bishops of the United States Speak Out

In May of 1983 the bishops of the United States issued their own pastoral letter on the issues that we face as one of the two powers capable of setting off a conflagration that could put an end to human life and civilization. The letter, *The Challenge of Peace: God's Promise and Our Response,* does not make for quick and easy reading for at least two reasons. First, the bishops face the whole range of complex issues related to nuclear weapons, both their possible use in war and their present use as a deterrence to war.

Second, the bishops are sensitive to where people are coming from. They recognize the difficulties faced by those in the armed forces who could be called upon to use weapons of mass destruction. They also recognize the dilemmas faced by those whose livelihood depends on working in weapons industries.

Further, while they painstakingly apply the traditional Catholic teaching on conditions for moral participation in war (that is, the *just-war* criteria), they also give their approval to the Catholic *nonviolent* position, seeing it as equally valid. In treating both these positions they insist over and over again that Catholics must labor to follow the injunction of the Second Vatican Council to evaluate war with an entirely new attitude. We need this new attitude, this fresh appraisal of war, because the advent of the atomic age in 1945 inaugurated a change in the nature of war, not merely a change in the means by which war is waged. Because it is of the utmost importance that American Catholics understand and respect these two approaches to moral issues of war, that is, just-war teaching and nonviolence, we quote the pastoral letter on this point:

> *While the just-war teaching has clearly been in possession for the past 1,500 years of Catholic thought, the "new moment" in which we find ourselves sees the just-war teaching and non-violence as distinct but interdependent methods of evaluating warfare. They diverge on some specific conclusions, but they share a*

common presumption against the use of force as a means of settling disputes.

Both find their roots in the Christian theological tradition; each contributes to the full moral vision we need in pursuit of a human peace. We believe the two perspectives support and complement one another, each preserving the other from distortion. Finally, in an age of technological warfare, analysis from the viewpoint of non-violence and analysis from the viewpoint of the just-war teaching often converge and agree in their opposition to methods of warfare which are in fact indistinguishable from total warfare. (The Challenge of Peace, 120-121)

A key fact to be kept in mind is that whenever the bishops use the term "total warfare," as in the passage just quoted, they refer to a kind of warfare that cannot be morally justified because it does not meet the just-war criteria.

The First Section of the Pastoral

The pastoral letter is divided into four main sections. **The first section** lays out religious perspectives and principles, drawing these from Sacred Scripture, both the Old Testament and the New Testament. The unifying symbol or idea is the kingdom of God, promised in the Old Testament, begun by Jesus, and to be brought to fulfillment by God's continuing saving action. We are reminded:

As disciples and as children of God, it is our task to seek for ways in which to make the forgiveness, justice and mercy, and love of God visible in a world where violence and enmity are too often the norm. When we listen to God's word, we hear again and always the call to repentance and to belief: to repentance because although we are redeemed we continue to need redemption; to belief, because although the reign of God is near, it is still seeking its fullness. (55)

It is in this section that the bishops explain both nonviolence and just-war teaching as "moral choices for the kingdom," noting that in both cases the presumption is against the use of armed force. The just-war teaching, however, gives us criteria for judging *when* a nation may go to war and also *how* the war must be conducted.

The Second Section of the Pastoral

The second section of the pastoral letter, which takes up specific problems of war in the technological age, has received the most attention. This section applies Catholic moral teaching to specific questions of U.S. military policy and to weapons systems now deployed as well as to other weapons and policies under consideration. The letter is careful to point out that the conclusions reached in this section do not have the same moral authority as universal moral principles. Nevertheless, the bishops present a carefully reasoned analysis and state their own conclusion. They approved the final draft of the letter by a vote of 238 to 9.

The bishops state that they see no circumstances under which nuclear weapons could be morally used, principally because nuclear war would violate the just-war principles of *discrimination* and *proportionality.* In just-war teaching, *discrimination* means that noncombatants may not be directly attacked. *Proportionality* demands that the evil inflicted must not outweigh the good achieved. (147-153)

The bishops plead for the formation of public opinion and official public policy which will reject any notion of a "winnable" nuclear war. They assert that nuclear weapons may not be used against cities in retaliation, even if the adversary uses nuclear weapons. They assert that the only moral stance toward nuclear war is to work for its prevention.

In examining *deterrence,* the bishops recognize that it is not a safe way to prevent war. They reject it as an end in itself or as a long-term strategy.

They further recognize that there are some Catholics, including some among their own number of bishops, who judge deterrence immoral: first, because it is a policy which threatens to use weapons which cannot be used morally; and second, because deterrence has not in fact set in motion substantial processes of disarmament. Nevertheless, on balance the bishops as a body hold to "a strictly conditioned moral acceptance of nuclear deterrence." They immediately add, "We cannot consider it adequate as a long-term basis for peace." (186)

The bishops state that they see no circumstances under which nuclear weapons could be morally used, principally because nuclear war would violate the just-war principles of *discrimination* and *proportionality.* In just-war teaching, *discrimination* means that noncombatants may not be directly attacked. *Proportionality* demands that the evil inflicted must not outweigh the good achieved.

This strictly conditioned moral acceptance is not to be interpreted as approval for every weapons system or policy advanced in the name of deterrence. On the contrary, it provides guidelines or criteria for judging specific policies. Thus, the bishops reject the quest for nuclear weapons superiority. (188) They reject first use of nuclear weapons in a war in which the adversary may have caused

> **On balance the bishops as a body hold to "a strictly conditioned moral acceptance of nuclear deterrence." They immediately add: "We cannot consider it adequate as a long-term basis for peace."**

great damage by conventional weapons. (150-156) They also reject first strike, that is, the use of nuclear weapons to incapacitate the adversary's nuclear arsenal.

The bishops recommend "support for immediate, bilateral, verifiable agreements to halt the testing, production, and deployment of new nuclear weapons systems." (191)

They further recommend support for negotiated bilateral deep cuts in the arsenals of both superpowers, support for early and successful conclusion of a comprehensive test ban treaty, removal by all parties of short-range nuclear weapons, and "removal by all parties of nuclear weapons from areas where they are likely to be overrun in the early stages of war, thus forcing rapid and uncontrollable decisions on their use." (191)

One of the aspects of the pastoral letter which has won it great respect, even among those who find its conclusions difficult to accept, is the evidence that the bishops did their homework over a two-year period, consulting with many experts in and out of government, and carefully studied and revised three drafts of the letter on the way to finally approving it. The group responsible for writing the text also went to Rome for a special meeting with Vatican officials and bishops from several European countries.

The Third Section of the Pastoral

The third section of the pastoral letter deals directly with the promotion of peace. The bishops echo the words of a well-known

American leader of the peace movement, A. J. Muste, who said, "There is no way to peace; peace is the way." Our bishops see "the building of peace as the way to prevent war." They call once more on the words of Pope John Paul II at Coventry Cathedral: "Peace is not just the absence of war. It involves mutual respect and confidence between peoples and nations. It involves collaboration and binding agreements. Like a cathedral, peace must be constructed patiently and with unshakable faith."

This section lays out short-range and long-range programs and goals for arms control and disarmament negotiations. (203-219) It also deals with efforts to develop nonviolent means of conflict resolution, urging that a percentage of the military budget be set aside to fund peace research. The bishops endorse the establishment of a national peace academy that would be on a par with the army, navy, and air force academies. (221-230) They also urge all Catholic educational institutions to develop peace education programs. They particularly call upon our Catholic universities to direct resources to peace education and research. (229-230)

This third section of the pastoral letter devotes considerable attention to the need for shaping international institutions for peace-keeping and for the promotion of an international world order that will respect universal human rights. The bishops speak strongly and clearly in support of the United Nations in this context, while acknowledging the need for its continuing development and also for reform of some of its structures and methods. They quote the words of Pope Paul VI to the U.N. General Assembly in 1965: "The edifice which you have constructed must never fail; it must be perfected and made equal to the needs which world history will present. You mark a stage in the development of mankind for which retreat must never be admitted, but from which it is necessary that advance be made."

The Fourth Section of the Pastoral

While the second and third sections of the pastoral letter are clearly intended as the bishops' contribution to the public debate on nuclear weapons and related issues, **the fourth and final section** speaks directly to the Catholic community. As in the first section, we are reminded once more of our discipleship, and that "to set out on the road to discipleship is to dispose oneself for a share in the cross."

It is in this section that the bishops call for *ongoing peace education in every diocese and parish,* asking that their pastoral letter "in its entirety, including its complexity, should be used as a guide and a framework. ... " (280)

It is also in this section that the bishops link issues of peace and war with the abortion issue, showing how their common element is in the attitude toward reverence for life. They remind us:

> *Abortion ... blunts a sense of the sacredness of human life. In a society where the innocent unborn are killed wantonly, how can we expect people to feel righteous revulsion at the act or threat of killing non-combatants in war? ...*
>
> *We must ask how long a nation willing to extend a constitutional guarantee to the "right" to kill de-fenseless human beings by abortion is likely to refrain from adopting strategic warfare policies deliberately designed to kill millions of defenseless human beings, if adopting them should come to seem "expedient."*
> (285-288)

In calling for prayer and penance, the pastoral letter urges a deepened understanding of the mystery of peace, expressed in the

---

The bishops urge all Catholic educational institutions to develop peace education programs. . . . they call for ongoing peace education in every diocese and parish. . . .

Eucharist, and calls for fasting, abstinence, and almsgiving for peace. The bishops publicly commit themselves to fasting and abstinence on Fridays.

> *As a tangible sign of our need and desire to do penance we, for the cause of peace, commit ourselves to fast and abstinence on each Friday of the year. We call upon our people voluntarily to do penance on Friday by eating less food and by abstaining from meat. This return to a traditional practice of penance, once well observed in the U.S. Church, should be accompanied by works of charity and service toward our neighbors. Every Friday should be a day significantly devoted to prayer, penance, and almsgiving for peace.* (298)

"We must ask how long a nation willing to extend a constitutional guarantee to the 'right' to kill defenseless human beings by abortion is likely to refrain from adopting strategic warfare policies deliberately designed to kill millions of defenseless human beings if adopting them should come to seem 'expedient.' "

Then the bishops turn to particular groups within the Catholic community who have specific responsibilities in the work for peace. Among these groups are parents, youth, men and women in military service and in defense industries, as well as priests and religious, educators, public officials, scientists, and those working with the media. Just before the section in which these groups are addressed, there is a word of "challenge and hope" to all Catholics. It is important because it makes very clear the posture we all need to adopt.

> *The arms race presents questions of conscience we may not evade. As American Catholics, we are called to express our loyalty to the deepest values we cherish: peace, justice and security for the entire human family. National goals and policies must be measured against that standard.*
>
> *We speak here in a specific way to the Catholic community. After the passage of nearly four decades and a concomitant growth in our understanding of the ever growing horror of nuclear war, we must shape the climate of opinion which will make it possible for our country to express profound sorrow over the atomic bombing in 1945. Without that sorrow, there is no possibility of finding a way to repudiate future use of nuclear weapons or of conventional weapons in such military actions as would not fulfill just-war criteria.* (301-302)

Finally, we are reminded of the source of our hope, Jesus, who died for us, who is risen and pleads for us.

> *It is our belief in the risen Christ which sustains us in confronting the awesome challenge of the nuclear arms race. Present in the beginning as the word of the Father, present in history as the word incarnate, and with us today in his word, sacraments, and spirit, he is the reason for our hope and faith. Respecting our freedom, he does not solve our problems but sustains us as we take responsibility for his work of creation and try to shape it in the ways of the kingdom. We believe his grace will never fail us.* (339)

Conclusion

For American Catholics, the first response to the teaching of the Church on the issues relating to nuclear weapons should be immense gratitude. The Church has not turned away from this most tormenting and terrifying issue. Rather, it has brought the riches of our faith to bear on it. Others beyond the Church have been inspired and encouraged by the pastoral letter of the American bishops. My own work in the peace movement took me to Europe four times in 1982, and everywhere I went I was asked about the pastoral letter our bishops were preparing.

It is clear that there are some fundamental differences between the positions of the U.S. Catholic hierarchy and those of the U.S. government on nuclear weapons issues, just as there are fundamental differences on the abortion issue. For individual Catholics this means that we must find a way to manage the tension between loyalty to country and resistance to some government policies. Beyond that, each of us needs to reflect carefully on our own responsibilities to make the teaching of the Church better known and to help shape a public climate and policy which will say a definite no to nuclear weapons, and which will insist on settling conflicts not by war but by the power of dialogue and sincere negotiations. With renewed conviction and commitment we accept the peace of Christ as our own gift and task. We trust in the power of his Spirit to help us bring our task to completion.

Points for Discussion

1. This chapter states that "The Church has never been silent on issues of peace and war." What are the three key ancient sources of Church teaching on the subject? What have popes and the Vatican said about it since World War II? (List the modern statements chronologically.)

2. List the teachings of the Second Vatican Council on war and peace which appear in this chapter.

3. In the first section of *The Challenge of Peace*, what do the bishops teach about: (a) the kingdom/reign of God; (b) the just-war criteria; (c) nonviolence; (d) what nonviolence and just-war teachings have in common; (e) general and selective conscientious objection?

4. In the second section of *The Challenge of Peace*, what do the bishops teach about: (a) nuclear weapons and the principles of *discrimination* and *proportionality*; (b) nuclear deterrence; (c) nuclear superiority; (d) first use of nuclear weapons; (e) first strike? What do the bishops recommend regarding: (f) the testing, the production, and the deployment of nuclear weapons; (g) deep cuts in superpower arsenals; (h) a comprehensive test ban treaty; (i) removal of short-range nuclear weapons; (j) removal of nuclear weapons from areas where they are likely to be overrun in early stages of war?

5. In the third section of *The Challenge of Peace*, what do the bishops say about: (a) developing means of nonviolent conflict resolution; (b) a national peace academy; (c) peace education in Catholic institutions; (d) U.N. work for human rights?

6. What does the fourth section of *The Challenge of Peace* say about: (a) abortion and nuclear war; (b) prayer, penance, and almsgiving for peace; (c) the arms race and American Catholics?

Recommended Reading

The Challenge of Peace: God's Promise and Our Response. Pastoral letter on war and peace by the U.S. Catholic bishops, issued on May 3, 1983. In the pastoral the bishops "urge every diocese and parish to implement balanced and objective educational programs to help people at all age levels to understand better the issues of war and peace ... during the next several years. To accomplish this, this pastoral letter in its entirety, including its complexity, should be used as a guide and a framework for such programs" (280). Order from Office of Publishing and Promotion Services, United States Catholic Conference, 1312 Massachusetts Avenue, N.W., Washington, D.C. 20005.

The Seamless Garment by Cardinal Joseph Bernardin. In his now-famous "Seamless Garment" speeches, Cardinal Bernardin of Chicago proposes that the "pro-life position of the Church must be developed in terms of a comprehensive and consistent ethic of life." His four speeches have been made into a booklet which is available from: *The Seamless Garment,* National Catholic Reporter, P.O. Box 281, Kansas City, MO 64141. Phone: 816/531-0538.

Part Two

Peacemaking in Our Lives

CHAPTER 4

Teaching Peace Through Our Everyday Lives

A teacher I know asked a class to make a list of the ten most precious things in the world or ten things they wanted most. Peace was on every student's list. Like those students, we know that if we lose our peace of mind or heart we have lost something invaluable. We will do almost anything to restore peace. If a country goes to war, people consider the situation tragic until there is peace once more. We recognize outstanding peacemakers as international heroes. One of the greatest honors a person can receive is the Nobel Peace Prize.

We do not need to consult a dictionary to recognize peace as the sum total of human goods. It is easy to grasp the *idea* of peace. What is difficult is to preserve peace when we have it or to restore it when it is broken or lost. This is true whether we are thinking about our own peace of heart, peace in a family, peace in a neighborhood, or peace between nations.

If we recall a failure to achieve peace in a serious situation, we are remembering a painful tragedy. On the other hand, if we remember being party to a reconciliation, we are bringing to mind an experience of deep joy. Even in small matters, a lack of peace entails anger, hurt, unhappiness, and a sense of failure. Peace, in contrast, always brings love, joy, happiness, and a general feeling of well-being and zest for life.

Jesus and Peace

In the Gospel of John, Jesus says to his disciples at the Last Supper, *"Peace I bequeath to you, my own peace I give you, a peace the*

73

world cannot give, this is my gift to you" (John 14:27). So, in our search for peace we want to be sure that we are doing all in our power to be open to the peace that is our Lord's *gift.*

But Jesus also said, *"Happy the peacemakers: they shall be called sons of God"* (Matthew 5:9). So peace is not only a gift from God, it is also a *task* we are to perform. It is a precious prize to be won by persevering efforts to live faithfully as followers of Jesus, learning from close association with him.

So far so good, we think. We are ready to work, even to sacrifice for peace in our lives and families. But what about *world* peace? What about the dangers of the arms race that could plunge the world into a final holocaust from which there would be no recovery? Can we do anything to reverse the spiral of violence that characterizes our world today?

Deep in our hearts we hunger to contribute to peacemaking in our world. But many people feel helpless before the magnitude of international problems. We pray for peace, knowing that a brief prayer is better than nothing, perhaps. But is that all there is to being a "peacemaker" as Jesus meant it?

In this chapter we want to examine our responsibilities and opportunities for peacemaking on all levels. Peace, especially world peace, is too important to be left only to those who hold political office. Our starting point must be the recognition that what government leaders can or cannot do depends on multitudes of persons like you and me. This is true because there can be genuine peace in society only when there is love and justice in those who make up society.

Yet, this is only half the story. Individuals often behave as they do because they express the expectations of the groups and institutions to which they belong. This is true of soldiers, nurses, newscasters, and teachers — to name only a few types. It is also true of playground bullies, gangsters, and those who torture political prisoners to obtain information. Individuals and groups or institutions have powerful mutual influence. So it is crucially important to support policies and institutions that are just and to work to change those that are unjust

74

and oppressive. In this sense the struggle for peace has necessarily a social and political dimension.

Peacemaking, then, requires lifelong effort on two levels: the *personal* and the *social* or *institutional.* We need to work at being just in our personal dealings because there is no peace without justice. But we also need to be vigilant and to call our government to account for policies of injustice toward any group or country.

Peace, especially world peace, is too important to be left only to those who hold political office. Our starting point must be the recognition that what government leaders can or cannot do depends on multitudes of persons like you and me.

The Catholic bishops of the United States gave us a splendid example of this kind of peacemaking in their 1983 pastoral letter, *The Challenge of Peace: God's Promise and Our Response.* They tell us very clearly that just as we cannot leave peace to the government neither may we leave it to the bishops themselves. They say: *"In a democracy, the responsibility of the nation and that of its citizens coincide."* (326) They also quote Pope John Paul at Hiroshima:

> *There is no justification for not raising the question of the responsibility of each nation and each individual in the face of possible wars and of the nuclear threat.*

To Reach Peace, Teach Peace

One practical way to assume our share of responsibility for peacemaking is to see ourselves as *teachers* of peace. Only a few will do their peace teaching in the classroom. For most of us the education we share together will take place in dozens of informal ways. We are called to hand on what we learn as close observers and companions of Jesus, who became our peace by giving his life on the Cross (Ephesians 2:14).

Individuals often behave as they do because they express the expectations of the groups and institutions to which they belong. So it is crucially important to support policies and institutions that are just and to work to change those that are unjust and oppressive.

In associating us with his life Jesus reconciles us with God, healing the wounds of sin and division. In his Spirit he gives us the power to reconcile, to forgive our enemies, even to lay down our lives for them. In the Eucharist he is the Lamb of God who takes away the sin of the world, the Lamb of God who grants us peace.

In *The Challenge of Peace,* our bishops leave no doubt about the source of our call to be peacemakers and the seriousness of that call. They say:

> *Peacemaking is not an optional commitment. It is a requirement of our faith. We are called to be peacemakers, not by some movement of the moment, but by our Lord Jesus.* (333)

Visions of Peace

On August 27, 1983, some 300,000 Americans held a peaceful march on Washington, under the slogan, "Jobs, Peace, and Freedom."

The date was the twentieth anniversary of the march on Washington where Martin Luther King, Jr., gave his historic "I Have a Dream" speech. Twenty years after that speech, speaker after speaker referred to the dream that has sustained black people and other minorities in their struggle for justice. The dream is also a vision of a possible future. Without it, spirits would lag and many would crumble under the weight and fatigue of the day-to-day labor for liberty and justice for all. *"Where there is no vision the people perish."* (Proverbs 29:18)

Few persons can stir the imagination of millions with the visionary power of a poet or great religious leader. All of us, however, have some capacity for sharing and handing on, even shaping a bit, the vision of such peacemakers as Martin Luther King, Gandhi, or Mother Teresa of Calcutta. Mother Teresa, who won the Nobel Peace Prize in 1979, has stirred the imagination of millions of people of all faiths by acting out her vision of a life spent doing "something beautiful for God." Her vision is one of ministering to Jesus in what she calls "his most distressing disguise," that of the helpless poor.

To bring visions of peace before our eyes we need to take time to see beneath the surface, to recognize that the important events in history are not wars and conquests. The important events are the multitude of humble actions which heal wounds and reconcile. We need to learn to reread history, recognizing that even in war it is the moments of relief from conflict which make possible the constructive works which endure. It is in this perspective that we get a sense of the great tasks that lie before us, the tasks of eradicating misery and constructing an international system which will judge all institutions and policies by their ability to contribute to the well-being of the one human family.

Concretely, this means that we should support our poets and artists. In the midst of the threat of global annihilation that hangs over us, they are the ones who can hold before us pictures of human possibility nurtured by love and hope. In this way the profound creative goodness, the energy of peace in the depths of each person, can be released and cultivated.

One person whose vision of peace still moves us after more than 700 years is Saint Francis of Assisi. Like Jesus' vision of peace, portrayed in the Sermon on the Mount, the vision of Francis is captured in a prayer. We know what we are up against and how we can make peace in the power of the Spirit when we pray:

> *Where there is hatred, let me sow love; where there is injury, pardon; where there is doubt, faith; where there is despair, hope; where there is darkness, light; where there is sadness, joy.*

Concrete Steps

In our time we have been called by the Second Vatican Council, and by our own bishops, *"to evaluate war with an entirely new attitude."* This means bringing the vision of peace to touch on the concrete realities of nuclear weapons technology and on the policies and strategies which accompany it. Our guiding vision must be of a world in which political conflicts are settled by dialogue and negotiation, not by war. We must free ourselves from the psychological shackles through which we view war as a tragic necessity. We must now come to see war as an unnecessary evil. In the words of Pope John Paul at Coventry Cathedral in 1982:

> *Today, the scale and the horror of modern warfare — whether nuclear or not — makes it totally unacceptable as a means of settling differences between nations. War should belong to the tragic past, to history; it should find no place on humanity's agenda for the future.*

In a vision of peace, a vision that can capture the imagination and win the allegiance of people today, what concrete reality is to replace war? How is a nation to defend its own people? To answer this question we need to do two things.

First, we need to reaffirm the view of human nature enshrined and expressed in Catholic tradition, a view which sees us as fundamentally good and rational at the core. True, we are sinners, and our political and social institutions bear marks of greed and selfishness. But persons and society are capable of being converted by the powerful love of God.

Second, we do well to reflect often on how that love of God, active in us, works to resolve most of our conflicts between persons and in social institutions. We resolve most of our conflicts nonviolently through dialogue and negotiation and — where necessary — through mediation, arbitration, and courts of law. It is only on the international scale that we still tolerate a kind of massive blood feud. To refuse to accept the truth that humane, nonviolent behavior can be raised to the level of international conduct is to despair of the practical goodness of God available to us who are made in his image and likeness.

Even more concretely, we need to envision the ways and means of active nonviolent defense and conflict resolution. It comes as a surprise to many people to learn that for years there has been on the drawing board a design for a United States Academy of Peace and Conflict Resolution. This academy, which has now been authorized by Congress, is meant to be the parallel to the national army, navy, and air force academies. This new academy will train professionals in the arts and skills of nonviolent conflict resolution. In their pastoral letter on peace, the U.S. bishops strongly endorse the establishment of such an academy, and further *"urge all citizens to support training in conflict resolution, non-violent resistance, and programs devoted to service to peace and education for peace."* (229)

The entire burden for training in nonviolent defense and conflict resolution, however, is not to be shifted to the newly established U.S. Institute of Peace. Our own Catholic educational institutions at all levels must take peace education seriously. The bishops call on

Catholic universities to develop programs for research, education, and training in peacemaking expertise.

Language of Peace

As we develop a vision of peace as possible, peace as urgent, peace as necessary for human survival, we will express this vision in a language of peace. Language, in turn, shapes our way of seeing things. The power of our own words to foster a climate of peace is simply amazing. Not a day passes without its opportunity to speak words of forgiveness and reconciliation, to support someone in a struggle to overcome prejudice and hostility, to help others see the possibility for a solution to the arms race through dialogue and negotiation. We can maximize our ability with words if we take time to become better informed on issues and write letters to editors, to our representatives in Congress, and to others in positions of influence.

On the negative side, careless use of language can condition us to see some persons as somehow less than fully human and therefore expendable. It is a well-known fact that efficiency in the wholesale killing that goes on in war depends on a conditioning by language. Soldiers are trained to see enemies as stripped of their full humanity rather than as brothers and sisters in the same human family. Yet, Jesus has made clear that in the Final Judgment he himself will tell us that whatever we did to another person, however labeled, we did to him.

The power of our own words to foster a climate of peace is simply amazing. Not a day passes without its opportunity to speak words of forgiveness and reconciliation, to support someone in a struggle to overcome prejudice and hostility.

In his first World Day of Peace message in 1979, Pope John Paul wrote a brilliant section on the relationship between language and peace. He said:

> *By expressing everything in terms of relations of force, of group and class struggles, and of friends and enemies, a propitious atmosphere is created for social barriers, contempt, even hatred and terrorism and underhanded or open support for them. On the other hand, a heart devoted to the higher value of peace produces a desire to listen and understand, respect for others, gentleness which is real strength, and trust. Such a language puts one on the path of objectivity, truth and peace.*

Gestures of Peace

Just as a vision of peace will find expression in the way we speak, so language will lead to action for peace. Here we will consider a few of the actions that are open to the great majority of us who do not hold positions of great political power. Our actions for peace — even when performed in a small arena — contribute to the climate which supports or prevents major political decisions which involve life and death.

• Our most constant opportunity for peacemaking behavior is in *caring* for all we meet and, therefore, in refusing to look upon anyone as an instrument for our own goals. This attitude of caring, which springs from a disposition of reverence, should extend also to the planet which is our home. Philosopher Milton Mayeroff has developed a philosophy around the notion of caring. His central premise is that a person is "at home" in the world not by dominating, nor even by understanding and appreciating, but by caring and being cared for. When we care for someone we find ways to work for that person's genuine good, and we bring out the best in that person.

Some of us who may never understand the complexities of military strategy can contribute mightily to a peaceful world by cultivating our capacity to care. We will not have to make elaborate plans to teach caring to our children if we practice it ourselves, because caring is highly contagious.

Our actions for peace — even when performed in a small arena — contribute to the climate which supports or prevents major political decisions which involve life and death.

• To *foster community* is another beautiful gesture of peace. A community is a group where all members share their joys, hopes, griefs, and anxieties. Where a community is centered in the experience of Jesus, who gives himself to us in word and sacrament, it will be quick to reach out to those who are in need. The works of Christian community are the corporal and spiritual works of mercy, the works of peace: *feed the hungry; give drink to the thirsty; clothe the naked; shelter the homeless; visit the sick; instruct the ignorant; counsel the doubtful* — and all the other works that express the vision of the kingdom of God and his justice and love.

• For some, and in times like ours we can expect the number to grow, one gesture of peace will take the form of *protest.* A person who strongly affirms human dignity and the right to life will experience a call to register objection to the use of nuclear weapons. This is precisely what happened to the American Catholic bishops. It is only a short step from protesting the use of weapons to protesting their manufacture. We may see a growing movement of support for those whose conscience leads them to give up jobs in weapons production, at considerable sacrifice for their families. With admirable pastoral sensitivity, our bishops speak to those in defense industries and also to us who know them as neighbors and fellow parishioners. The bishops say:

> *Those who in conscience decide that they should no longer be associated with defense activities should find support in the Catholic community. Those who remain in these industries or earn a profit from the weapons industry should find in the Church guidance and support for the ongoing evaluation of their work.* (318)

• Another peacemaking gesture is anything that helps us understand and appreciate those whose ways are different from ours. In the 1982 World Day of Peace message, "Peace: A Gift of God Entrusted to Us," Pope John Paul encouraged cultural exchanges. He noted:

> *Anything that enables people to get to know each other better through artistic activity breaks down barriers. Where speech is unavailing and diplomacy is an uncertain aid, music, painting, drama and sport can bring people closer together. The same holds for scientific research: Science, like art, creates and brings together a universal society which gathers all who love truth and beauty, without division. Thus science and art are, each at its own level, an anticipation of the emergence of a universal peaceful society.*

• The most beautiful and powerful gesture of peace, and the one that Jesus called his new commandment, is to *love our enemies* (see Luke 6:27-35). In loving and forgiving those who denied, betrayed, tortured, and killed him, Jesus revealed for all time the full potential of humanity. It is possible that in our own day we are beginning to come to grips with the mystery of *unconditional love* as the *central condition of peace,* the peace that Jesus gives us both as gift and as task.

Conclusion

There is no doubt that peacemaking has taken on a new urgency in our time. We now know that we must put an end to war, or war will put an end to us. In this chapter we have looked at ways of linking our personal peacemaking efforts to the historic challenge to create a world freed from the terror of nuclear weaponry. As the American bishops have told us most solemnly, peacemaking is not an option.

In loving and forgiving those who tortured and killed him, Jesus revealed the full potential of humanity. We may be beginning to come to grips with the mystery of *unconditional love* as the *central condition of peace,* the peace that Jesus gives us both as gift and as task.

We are called to cultivate hope-filled *visions* of peace, a peace that God wants to give us with an intense desire beyond our imagining. We can help shape peace by our *language* and by the many *gestures* open to us. We can trust that as we are faithful to the opportunities that present themselves day by day, God will shape our hearts, enlighten our minds, and lead us further on the path of peace.

Below are organizations whose members strive to reach peace by teaching peace. You may want to write for further information to:

Pax Christi USA, 348 E. 10th Street, Erie, PA 16503. This is the American branch of the international Catholic peace movement. Members follow a program of prayer, study, and action. They work for peace for humankind, witnessing to the peace of Christ. Members are encouraged to form local and regional groups. A regular newsletter keeps them in touch with the national group.

Fellowship of Reconciliation, Box 271, Nyack, NY 10960. The American Fellowship is part of an international interfaith peace movement founded in 1914. Its members are committed to experimenting with the power of love and truth in solving human conflict. The magazine *Fellowship* is a very useful resource.

National Peace Institute Foundation, 110 Maryland Avenue, N.E., Suite 409, Washington, D.C. 20002. This foundation provides information on the U.S. Institute of Peace established by Congress in 1984.

Points for Discussion

1. This chapter remarks that "Individuals and groups often behave as they do because they express the expectations of the groups and institutions to which they belong." Give examples of this point in areas such as (a) race relations, (b) alcohol and tobacco consumption, (c) the way people speak and vote about issues of peace and national security. How does this tie in with the need to work for justice in policies and institutions?

2. Drawing from the section entitled "Visions of Peace" in this chapter, compose a statement that expresses your own "Vision of Peace."

3. List some common slogans and names that create antipathy between groups in our society. Suggest ways we can use language to create positive rapport between (a) races, (b) religions, (c) the sexes, (d) the superpowers.

4. Using the sections entitled "Gestures of Peace" and "Conclusion" in this chapter, make a list of actions that you plan to work into your everyday life.

Recommended Reading

The Bible, the Church, and Social Justice by Richard Schiblin, C.SS.R. Liguori Publications, 1983. Paperback. $1.50.

Peace: A Moral Issue for Women? by Suzanne Hagan. Liguori Publications, 1983. 50¢ pamphlet.

Prejudice: What You Can Do About It by Charles DeCelles, Ph.D. Liguori Publications, 1983. 50¢ pamphlet.

CHAPTER 5

Teaching Our Children to Be Peacemakers

As our understanding of the nuclear threat grows, so does our concern about our children. There is no way we can shield them from awareness of the devastating power of nuclear weapons. At the same time, we cannot know what children are going through, what it means to be growing up in the age of overkill, because our own childhood was lived in very different circumstances.

Even though the atomic bomb has been with us for nearly forty years, it is only recently that the arms race has been widely recognized for what it is — a "machine gone mad." Those descriptive words are from a statement of the Holy See to the Secretary General of the United Nations in 1976. In 1983, Pope John Paul II spoke of humanity as "this great patient in danger of death."

Psychologists, in trying to find an adequate description for the effect of our situation, speak of "nuclear numbing." We know that numbing, paralyzing fear is not good for children; as responsible adults we need to find ways to counteract it.

All adults share in the responsibility to help reverse our present tragic situation. The best way to overcome the numbing fear which characterizes our society is to take seriously the words of Jesus, *"Happy the peacemakers. . . . "* (Matthew 5:9) In peacemaking we express the love that casts out fear. We will be able to educate our children and young people in ways of peace to the extent that we ourselves have a clear understanding and a steadfast position regarding peace and war.

This chapter situates our effort within the broad sweep of history, discusses what we should teach our children, and suggests some specific actions.

Where in the World Are We?

Over the course of history, what is it that distinguishes civilization from barbarism? Historians tell us it is the public will to take care of the "widow and the orphan," a term that stands for all those who cannot make it on their own. In the Hebrew tradition we find this concern expressed over and over again in the pages of the Old Testament.

The history of the Church shows the development of this tradition, inspired and sustained by the life and words of Jesus. For example, Christians were pioneers in the development of schools and hospitals. In the Acts of the Apostles we read that deacons were appointed to take care of distributing food to the needy. (Read, for example, Acts 2:42-47 and 4:32-35.) In Europe the earliest schools were attached to monasteries.

There is no way we can shield our children from the awareness of nuclear weapons. We cannot know what children are going through, what it means to be growing up in the age of overkill. . . .

Today, war and the preparation for war have so violated the tradition of care for the poor and the vulnerable that we are in danger of losing the very principle and ideal which is at the heart of civilization.

In World War II, civilian deaths far outnumbered military casualties. Today there are some eight million refugees in the world, mostly women and children, victims of past and present wars. Today's nuclear weapons make a mockery of concern for children, the sick, and the elderly. The bishops at the Second Vatican Council strongly condemned the indiscriminate killing by conventional weapons as well as nuclear weapons in these words:

> *Any act of war aimed indiscriminately at the destruction of entire cities or of extensive areas along with their population is a crime against God and man himself. It merits unequivocal and unhesitating condemnation.* (Church in the Modern World, 80)

Attitudes Toward Life

Our bishops speak of ours as a time of supreme crisis. In this situation the young will be only as secure as we are. With unfailing intuition, they can tell whether we are confused, despondent, cynical, or calloused about the world situation today. As educators for peace, therefore, we do well to begin with the following questions to ourselves:

• Do we take sufficient time to nourish our faith and confidence in the goodness and providence of God as we experience that loving providence in our own lives?

• Do we welcome life each day in gratitude, cherishing it as a great gift entrusted to us?

• Do we reverence all human life, whether in the womb, in a refugee camp, or perhaps in a child or young person who is afraid that there may be no world to grow up in?

• Remembering that we are called to be peacemakers, do we consistently work for reconciliation wherever peace is lacking?

In the Summary of their 1983 pastoral letter, *The Challenge of Peace: God's Promise and Our Response,* the American bishops tell us:

> *Peacemaking is not an optional commitment. It is a requirement of our faith. We are called to be peacemakers, not by some movement of the moment, but by our Lord Jesus. The content and context of our peacemaking is set not by some political agenda or ideological program, but by the teaching of his Church.*

We give an unmistakable witness to faith, hope, and love by engaging in works of peacemaking on the personal level. We also witness as citizens helping to shape public policy. Further on in this chapter there are suggestions for concrete actions we can take. But before we involve ourselves through action, it is important to commit ourselves firmly to the way of the Gospel. Otherwise, we run the risk of misdirected efforts and of discouragement when we do not see immediate results. *The Challenge of Peace* reminds us that as a community of disciples of Jesus we must support one another. "We must develop a sense of solidarity, cemented by relationships with mature and exemplary Christians who represent Christ and his way of life." (277)

What to Teach

We need to teach our children at all age levels that we are living at a turning point in history. This is a time when the human family must refuse to give legal sanction to war. It is good to remind ourselves that flogging and slavery were once legal, and even considered morally tolerable. There is no legal support for such practices today.

Withdrawing legal and social approval for war does not mean that the world would be entirely free of terrorism or acts of aggression. It does mean that governments would have to invest far more seriously in alternatives to war. Such alternatives exist, but they have not yet been tried consistently by major states. Under today's conditions in which military technology has given us instruments for mutual suicide, we need to train people professionally in the arts and skills of reconciliation, diplomacy, dialogue, mediation, and arbitration.

The best way to overcome the numbing fear that characterizes our society is to take seriously the words of Jesus, "Blessed the peacemakers." In peacemaking we express the love that casts out fear.

Reliance on war as a final resort in international conflicts has brought us to the point of risking national and global suicide. Nevertheless, as peace researcher Michael Nagler has commented, we will not discard war until we see some convincing alternatives. These alternatives exist and can be grouped in three categories. All have been successfully tried, and they now await adoption as ways of national and international policy. The three categories of alternatives to violence are:

1. the creation of social structures that do not breed criminality, economic structures that do not exploit the poor, and national policies that do not create hostility;

2. development of strategies for resolving conflicts when they do occur, such as mediation by third parties and negotiation;

3. measures of last resort, such as nonviolent civilian-based defense, by which armed invasions have been neutralized, frustrated, and defused.

National Peace Academy

To train professional peacemakers, we need a United States Peace Academy possessing as much government support as that given to our military, naval, and air force academies. Such an academy is not a new idea. For years a small group of people have been working on its design.

In 1981, the Commission on Proposals for the National Academy of Peace and Conflict Resolution recommended the establishment of a U.S. Academy of Peace. The commission found that "peace is a legitimate field of learning that encompasses rigorous, inter-disciplinary research, education, and training directed toward peacemaking expertise."

Our United States bishops strongly support the Peace Academy. In their 1983 pastoral letter, they say: "We endorse the commission's recommendation and urge all citizens to support training in conflict resolution, non-violent resistance, and programs devoted to service to peace and education for peace. Such an academy would not only provide a center for peace studies and activities, but also be a tangible evidence of our nation's sincerity in its often professed commitment to international peace and the abolition of war." (229)

Late in 1984, Congress finally authorized $16 million for the Peace Academy, which will now be known officially as the U.S. Institute of Peace. A Washington-based office — the National Peace Institute Foundation — will continue to educate citizens about the development of this new Institute. The Institute can become a powerful and constructive force for good. We need to make our government know that we want the U.S. Institute of Peace to develop quickly into an outstanding institute of higher learning.

Works of Mercy — Works of Peace

Our clear ideas and convictions about alternatives to violence need to be grounded in faith in the basic goodness of human nature, a goodness which is more fundamental than our tendencies to sin. Our goodness is not our achievement, it is a gift from God. We are a people redeemed by a loving God who did not spare his only Son to redeem us from error, sin, and death. It is in a spirit of gratitude and with enthusiasm born of faith and hope that we undertake the works of peace, which are the most effective way of preventing war.

These works of peace have been traditionally known as the works of mercy. Today we need them more than ever before, and we need to recognize explicitly that they are *works of peace.* How can we best teach Christian peacemaking to our children? We can teach them peace by working together with them in actual peacemaking activities adapted to their level of emotional, intellectual, and social development. A family, a parish, even an entire diocese can make a careful and concerted effort to build peace through these corporal and spiritual works of mercy:

Corporal Works of Mercy	Spiritual Works of Mercy
Feed the hungry	Instruct the ignorant
Give drink to the thirsty	Counsel the doubtful
Clothe the naked	Admonish the sinner
Visit those in prison	Comfort the sorrowful
Shelter the homeless	Bear wrongs patiently
Visit the sick	Forgive all injuries
Bury the dead	Pray for the living and the dead

How can we best teach Christian peacemaking to our children? We can teach them peace by working together with them in actual peacemaking activities, the corporal and spiritual works of mercy.

Jobs, Careers for Peace

One of the most important responsibilities toward young people is to help them make decisions about their vocations, jobs, professions, and careers. Here we can learn from a recent address of Pope John Paul to the Pontifical Academy of Sciences, an international group of seventy eminent scientists, twenty of whom are Nobel Prize winners. The Pope made explicit reference to the relationship between scientific research and war preparation when he said:

> *When, in a particular historical situation, it is all but inevitable that a certain form of scientific research will be used for purposes of aggression, he (the scientist) must make a choice that will enable him to work for the good of people, for the building up of peace.*
>
> *By refusing certain fields of research, inevitably destined, in the concrete historical circumstances, for deadly purposes, the scientists of the whole world ought to be united in a common readiness to disarm science and to form a providential force for peace.*

We must not let our young people simply drift into occupations which contribute to the preparation for violence which characterizes our times. A key situation for vocational and career guidance is the question of military training. In this matter we should not wait until the week before a man's eighteenth birthday, when he is required to register for a possible military draft. Nor should we exclude young women from our educational efforts regarding military service. All Catholics should know the teaching of the Church on this topic as interpreted by our own bishops for the American situation. In their 1983 pastoral letter on peace and war, the U.S. bishops speak both of the responsibilities of those in military service, and of the right of conscientious objection and the Church's support of that right. We can make the words of our bishops to youth our own:

> *We call you to choose your future work and professions carefully. How you spend the rest of your lives will determine, in large part, whether there will any longer be a world as we know it. We ask you to study carefully the teachings of the Church and the demands of the gospel about war and peace. We encourage you to seek careful guidance as you reach conscientious decisions about your civic responsibilities in this age of nuclear military forces.* (307)

Our responsibilities toward the young do not end with helping them find their own conscientious position regarding nuclear weapons and war. In the long run, it is even more important to help them commit themselves to the positive work of peacemaking. Below are some suggestions that can help them, and us, set our feet firmly on the path of peace.

One of our most important responsibilities toward young people is to help them make decisions about their vocations, jobs, professions, and careers. We must not let our young people simply drift into occupations which contribute to the preparation for violence which characterizes our time.

Suggested Activities

• Listen carefully to children and young people as they express their fears, ideas, and concerns about war, the nuclear threat, and other kinds of violence. Be available to them, generous with your time and concern. If you are not able to answer a question on the spot, be sure the young person knows your concern. Set aside a definite time to discuss the situation later. Psychologists tell us that while young people have always felt their security threatened by violence, ours is the first generation in which young people feel that the adults have lost their grip, especially in the area of international affairs. We need to be especially attentive to small children and to those who are shy, who may be suffering from extreme fear and unable to express themselves.

• Share your own faith with children. In the family and in classroom settings, talk about the way of Jesus and his teachings on love and nonviolence. Plan simple activities which carry out works of mercy, and help children see that these are at the same time works of peace.

• Become a member of a peace movement which can be an important support system for your own efforts to deepen both your faith commitment and your activities. In addition to the organizations listed on pages 84 and 85 in the previous chapter, here is one specifically for families: *Parenting for Peace and Justice*, 4144 Lindell Blvd., St. Louis, MO 63108. This national network helps families to integrate family life and social ministry. A quarterly newsletter provides practical suggestions and gives information about new resources and programs for families.

We need to be especially attentive to small children and to those who are shy, who may be suffering from extreme fear and unable to express themselves.

• Welcome and encourage the participation of young people in your own peacemaking activities.

● Have children learn about outstanding peacemakers. *The Challenge of Peace* mentions Saint Francis of Assisi, Gandhi, Martin Luther King, and Dorothy Day. See that your school and local library have suitable reading material on each of these peacemakers.

● Study the section on prayer and penance in *The Challenge of Peace* and then discuss what this sentence can mean in your family: *"Every Friday should be a day significantly devoted to prayer, penance, and almsgiving for peace."* (298)

● Use the Peace Prayer of Saint Francis in your family. Someone in the family might make a beautiful copy of the prayer for a special place in your home.

Peace Prayer of Saint Francis

O Lord, make me an instrument
*   of your peace.*
Where there is hatred,
*   let me sow love,*
Where there is injury, pardon,
Where there is doubt, faith,
Where there is despair,
*   let me bring hope,*
Where there is darkness, light,
And where there is sadness, joy.
O Divine Master,
*   grant that I may not so much seek*
To be consoled as to console,
To be understood as to understand,
To be loved as to love.
For it is in giving that we receive,
It is in pardoning that we are pardoned,
And it is in dying that we are born
*   to eternal life.*

Points for Discussion

1. In the section entitled "Where in the World Are We?" this chapter offers four questions about basic attitudes and actions. Explore these questions one by one.

2. Using the traditional Works of Mercy listed in this chapter, write down some practical "Works of Peace" geared to the age level of the children with whom you live.

3. Draw up a written plan outlining how you can make the "Suggested Activities" in this chapter part of your own family life.

Recommended Reading

Parenting for Peace and Justice by Kathleen McGinnis and James McGinnis. Orbis Books, 1981. Paperback. This book offers many practical suggestions and resources for nurturing family involvement in the works of justice and peace.

CHAPTER 6

Practical Ways to
Turn Bombs into Bread

God and Economics

All of us have had experience in making a budget of some kind, formally or informally. Basically, a budget is a plan, a forecast of the way we intend to use our money and other resources. At first sight a budget may not seem "spiritual." In fact, it is one acid test of where our heart is.

Jesus himself is remembered as speaking of budgetary matters as lessons in the spiritual life. There is the story of the foolish man who kept enlarging his barns to store his surplus harvest, only to die before he could use his goods. He is called a fool (Luke 12:13-21). Or, there is the man who buried his treasure instead of investing it (Matthew 25:14-30) or the man who had to sit down and figure out his assets before beginning to build a home (Luke 14:28-33).

Today government budgets worldwide are badly askew. In developed and developing countries alike, one item of the budget has risen astronomically since 1945. That item is armaments. Since the end of World War II, first a creeping and now a galloping militarization has taken over our planet. We have become accustomed to the term "arms race" and, by now, may see it as normal.

In this chapter we will examine the trade-offs governments make in allocating more and more resources to arms and less and less to basic social needs, such as health care and education. We will then be in a better position to answer this fundamental question:

Can we continue the arms race at its present rate without sacrificing in the process the very lives we mean to protect and defend?

The Church and the Arms Race

The present arms race has been a deep concern of the Church long before it reached its present epidemic proportions. The Second Vatican Council's Pastoral Constitution on the Church in the Modern World (1965) points out the moral dimension of the economics of the arms race:

While extravagant sums are being spent for the furnishing of ever new weapons, an adequate remedy cannot be provided for the multiple miseries afflicting the whole modern world. Disagreements between nations are not really and radically healed. On the contrary other parts of the world are infected with them. New approaches initiated by reformed attitudes must be adopted to remove this trap and to restore genuine peace by emancipating the world from its crushing anxiety.

Therefore, it must be said again: the arms race is an utterly treacherous trap for humanity, and one which injures the poor to an intolerable degree. It is much to be feared that if this race persists, it will eventually spawn all the lethal ruin whose path it is now making ready. (81)

With this background in the teaching of the Church on the arms race, we turn to a consideration of the economic facts. While the arms race accelerates, how is the human family doing in its ability to provide food, clothing, and shelter for all God's children?

Economic Trade-offs

More than 15 million children die each year for lack of food and inexpensive vaccines. Broken down into numbers we can manage, this means over 43,000 children a day, or 30 each minute. To bring this horror home, I find it useful, and painful, to picture a classroom of 30 children I have taught, and to picture them dead, victims of poverty's diseases. Then I multiply by 60, to reach 1,800 dead children an hour. Then I multiply by 24, to come to 43,200 children a day. Already I find it difficult to imagine such a crowd of children. Finally, I multiply by 365 to bring the total to 15,768,000 a year.

More than any statistic I know, the destruction of children by hunger and preventable disease cuts into my conscience and refuses to allow me to go on with business as usual. Businesses as usual absorb 1.3 million dollars a minute of public money for military purposes. A tiny fraction of the arms budget, a budget in which there is scandalous waste, could save the children now, by providing essential food and medicine.

A budget is a plan of the way we intend to use our money and resources. A budget is spiritual — an acid test of where our heart is.

The cost of military defense per person in the United States is today more than ten times what it was just before World War II. Let's take another example of an economic trade-off we are making. Although we now have enough firepower to destroy the world and many more planets if they were within range of our warheads, we continue to make nuclear submarines at enormous cost. How enormous? If we cancelled only *one* of these submarines, the money saved would equal the annual education budget of 23 developing countries with 160 million school-age children.

More than 15 million children die each year for lack of food and inexpensive vaccines — over 43,000 children a day, or 30 each minute.

What Race Are We Winning?

One way to assess the economic consequences of the arms race for the United States is to compare the U.S. economy with that of other industrialized nations. Here the picture is particularly alarming. In the last several years the United States has spent more than twice as much on military as on civilian research. In the European community, on the other hand, the proportions are exactly the reverse: over twice as much public money has gone to civilian as to military research.

In a study ranking the United States with twelve other wealthy countries, including ten in Western Europe, Japan, and Canada, for the years 1960-1979, the United States comes out first in defense expenditures and tenth in average annual real growth in domestic product. The two countries with the worst economic growth records from 1960-1980 — the United States and Great Britain — were the two countries devoting the largest proportion of their gross national product to military spending. The countries with the better growth rates spent less on the military. Japan, which spent least on the military, had an economic growth rate well over twice that of the United States.

John Kenneth Galbraith, the well-known Harvard economist, has been pointing out the adverse economic effect of concentrating our capital on development of military technology, on which we spend ten times as much as the Japanese. Over sixty percent of federal research and development funds in the U.S. are concentrated on defense. Japan, meanwhile, applies its best scientific talents and government funds to build better autos, televisions, and computers.

In the words of economist Lester Thurow, "While the Japanese are busy working on their fifth generation computer, we're busy building the MX."

There is now widespread agreement among economists that defense spending does not provide the jobs it promises. Defense industries provide highly paid and highly skilled jobs for scientists and engineers, but comparatively few for those who will never qualify for such jobs. The Council on Economic Priorities estimates that each $1 billion spent on the controversial MX missile provides 53,000 direct and indirect jobs. That may look good — but not after we learn that the same $1 billion would produce 77,000 jobs in mass transit and 69,000 in housing.

Another study of the effect of government spending on creating jobs concludes that $1 billion spent by the Pentagon creates roughly 48,000 jobs — but $1 billion spent in other ways would create 76,000 jobs in sewer construction, 77,000 jobs in nursing, and 100,000 jobs in teaching.

We need to keep in mind, of course, that a job is not an end in itself. Even if the Pentagon could wipe out unemployment instead of contributing to it, as is actually the case, we would have to ask the fundamental moral question about what people are doing on their jobs. That brings us to a consideration of the social consequences of the arms race.

Arms and the Quality of Life

The high cost of the arms race cannot be measured only in economic terms. We need to face the social consequences, which are no less real even if they cannot be expressed in dollars and cents. Since 1978, statistics have been available which rank the countries of the world in military expenditures and also in such indicators of social standing as per capita income, school-age population per teacher, population per physician, infant mortality rate, and life expectancy. Many Americans presume that the United States is a superpower in all these indicators, and they are surprised at the following chart, listing rank of the United States among 141 countries in 1980.

Military expenditures	1
Per capita income	16
School-age population per teacher	7
Percent of women in university enrollment	12
Population per physician	26
Infant mortality rate	19
Life expectancy	8

Worldwide, the picture is so bleak that many people prefer not to face it. Ruth Leger Sivard, in the highly respected annual study *World Military and Social Expenditures,* points out that

— in 1983 young men in twenty-five countries were eligible to go to war at an earlier age than they were eligible to vote;

— the U.S. now devotes $200 billion a year to foreign enemies, but forty-five percent of Americans are afraid to go out alone at night within one mile of their homes;

Economists agree that defense spending does not provide the jobs it promises. Defense industries provide highly paid jobs for scientists and engineers, but comparatively few for others.

— the world's stockpile of nuclear weapons represents an explosive force over 5,000 times greater than all the munitions used in World War II.

Disastrous Results

One result is that the youth of the world see their elders as out of touch with reality and the political process out of control.

The arms race has not prevented smaller wars. Since 1945, the arms race is connected to a cancerous arms trade, providing hundreds of countries with the wherewithal to try to settle their differences by military means. The consequence of resorting to war has been sixteen million war-related deaths since 1945. Many more of these deaths are among civilians than among the armed forces involved.

The increasing militarization of our planet has also made ours the century of refugees. Conservative estimates put the number of refugees in 1983 at eight million. By far the greatest number are women and children.

The greater availability of modern weapons throughout the world has gone hand in hand with the increase in the most extreme forms of systematic political terrorism. Amnesty International says that the use of torture as a political instrument has reached epidemic proportions. Many governments today are using arms and torture to repress the very people they are supposed to defend. In 1983 there were eighty-three countries reported to have used violence against the public in the form of torture, brutality, and summary executions. Forty-eight of these countries appear to resort to these uses of violence frequently.

What is striking is that among the countries most prone to use torture, three-fourths have military-controlled governments. Almost all of the worst offenders are clients of the U.S. or U.S.S.R. and are large importers of the equipment which represents the most advanced "repressive technology."

At the same time that military sales and military aid to poor countries have skyrocketed, economic aid for these same countries has been stingy. Many people are unaware that by far the largest proportion of foreign aid is military. In 1982, military expenditures of the economically developed countries were seventeen times larger than their economic aid to foreign countries.

Many governments are using arms and torture to repress the very people they are supposed to defend.

Weapons Are Already Destroying Us

This is tragic in a world in which all nations are so economically interdependent for raw materials and technology. Perhaps the most important lesson of the second half of the twentieth century is that we must all flourish or languish together. *The arms race and the arms trade it fuels are destroying the social fabric of the world, even if the nuclear weapons are never fired.* Intelligent investments in genuine human development, on the contrary, would be returned many times over in enlarged markets and a mutual stake in peaceful coexistence.

Even more than in countries like our own, in poor countries investment in the military sector is at the price of terrible social neglect. At least one person in five in our world today is trapped in absolute poverty. More and more we are coming to see this level of destitution as silent genocide. Eleven million babies a year die before their first birthday. As of 1980, less than ten percent of children in the Third World were being immunized against the six common diseases of childhood. Five million were killed by these diseases yearly. It is a cruel lie to tell the parents of such children that the latest in military technology is defending them against outside aggression.

The number of illiterates in the world is growing, not diminishing, and is growing at a faster rate among females than among males. There are in our world today 120 million young children of school age who have no school they can go to.

A Time of Moral Confusion

Historians looking back on the present period between 1945 and the 1980s may well characterize this as a time of intellectual and moral confusion. It is now clear that the trauma of the use of atomic weapons on Hiroshima and Nagasaki in 1945 threw the world into a state of bewilderment about the very important issue of political and social security. As Einstein correctly observed, the atomic bomb changed everything but our way of thinking. By and large, people of all political persuasions have continued to assume that settling international disputes by war is evil but, somehow, at times inevitable.

Under the impact of the nuclear threat, we are slowly coming to the realization that war is an unnecessary evil. It is a human invention. The same human beings who invented war can invent alternatives to it, and must, if the human race is to survive.

A consideration of the economic and social cost of war does not of itself provide the strongest arguments against war. Nevertheless, such a consideration can be a necessary part of a growing conviction that we must resist the cancerous growth of militarism that characterizes our period of history. The world has become an armed camp in which deaths from social neglect, war, political repression, and torture have come to be taken for granted.

To accept such a situation as inevitable would be to contribute to the brutalizing of the human spirit. More than ever we need to strengthen our faith in the goodness which is ours because we are made in the image of God. We are called to share God's very life as one family, living in peace, a peace grounded in the love that hungers and thirsts for justice.

Even worse than physical death from nuclear weapons would be the spiritual death of despair, crumbling before the pressures of violence that have grown to such enormous proportions in our day.

The arms race and the arms trade it fuels are destroying the social fabric of the world, even if the nuclear weapons are never fired.

What Can We Do?

• *We can use our power as citizens to monitor the federal budget.* At the November 1983 meeting of the National Conference of Catholic Bishops, Bishop Peter Rosazza, auxiliary of Hartford, Connecticut, urged the group to set up a "monitoring committee" to follow U.S. defense developments more closely. We can show our support for this endeavor, and also make our own voices heard, by visits to our Congressional representatives and by letters to them and to the editors of our newspapers.

• *We can help spread the teaching of the Church on the arms race and the arms trade.* In their 1983 pastoral letter on peace and war, our bishops addressed these issues. We should make it our own responsibility to study their teaching. On November 12, 1983, Pope John Paul made his most forceful statement to date on nuclear arms when he addressed the Pontifical Academy of Sciences. His audience of seventy eminent scientists included twenty Nobel Prize winners. Pope John Paul spoke of the urgency of rescuing science from its service to the arms buildup "so that the factories of death may give place to laboratories of life." He said further, "By refusing certain fields of research, inevitably destined, in the concrete historical circumstances, for deadly purposes, the scientists of the whole world ought to be united in a common readiness to disarm science and to form a providential force for peace."

• *We can make career choices that foster peace, and help the young in their choices.* The words of Pope John Paul to scientists can be applied to many others involved one way or another in arms manufacture. All Christians need to examine their work carefully. In *The Challenge of Peace,* their pastoral letter on peace and war, our American bishops have a special word for those in defense industries, telling them that they should find in the Church "guidance and support for the ongoing evaluation of their work."

• *We can give moral support and, where needed, material support to those who for reasons of conscience have given up jobs or careers in arms-related works.* In the diocese of Amarillo, Texas, a counseling service is available to such persons. More such services are needed throughout the country.

• *We can stand on the side of the poor in the struggle to achieve justice.* To do this we will need to take time to study political issues, and to give our support to those in public life who resist the increasing militarization of our planet and who foster policies and programs designed to provide the necessities of life to all. A high priority should be full employment and a continuing evaluation of the nature of the jobs available. We should never succumb to the mistaken notion that we need a swollen defense industry to create jobs.

At least one person in five in our world is trapped in absolute poverty. More and more we are coming to see this as silent genocide. Eleven million babies a year die before their first birthday.

• *We can pray with love and perseverance for those in power whose decisions contribute to the arms race and the arms trade.* The present and future safety of the entire human family depend on the actions of people in high places. We pray that they will come to see that a spiraling arms race can destroy all those who participate in it, as well as those who are the direct and indirect victims of it. Our persevering prayer is a test of our own faith, hope, and love.

Points for Discussion

1. Using Luke 12:13-21, Luke 14:28-33, and Matthew 25:14-30, discuss reasons why budgeting is a spiritual activity.

2. The question asked early in this chapter is: *Can we continue the arms race at its present rate without sacrificing in the process the very lives we mean to protect and defend?* Taking them one by one, review each of the following sections in this chapter. At the end of each section, stop and answer the original question with a yes or a no. The sections are titled: (a) "Economic Trade-offs"; (b) "What Race Are We Winning?"; (c) "Arms and the Quality of Life"; (d) "Disastrous Results"; (e) "Weapons Are Already Destroying Us."

3. The section "What Can We Do?" offers six suggestions. Discuss each point and formulate some practical activities that are within your capabilities.

Recommended Reading

World Military and Social Expenditures by Ruth Leger Sivard. Much of the material in this chapter is based on this classic work which is updated annually. You can order the latest edition from World Affairs Bookstore, 421 South Wabash Avenue, Chicago, IL 60605. Phone: 312/663-4250.

CHAPTER 7

Four Ways You Can Help Hungry People

Christ in Disguise

There is perhaps no passage in the Gospels which stirs us more deeply than Saint Matthew's account of the Last Judgment. In the mysterious story of the king who will gather all the nations before him, separating good from bad as a shepherd separates sheep from goats, Jesus gave us his own vision of the meaning of human life. What matters in the end is love expressed in action for those in need. Jesus accepts as done to himself whatever we do to our neighbor.

> *Come, you whom my Father has blessed. ... For I was hungry and you gave me food. ... Go away from me. ... For I was hungry and you never gave me food.* (Matthew 25:34,35,41,42)

With good reason we cannot be indifferent to anyone who lacks the necessities of life. As our knowledge and love of God grow, so does our concern to respond as fully as we can to Jesus in what Mother Teresa of Calcutta calls "his most distressing disguise."

I once had an opportunity to ask Mother Teresa a question that had been nagging at me. How could I, who am going through life well-fed and well-clothed, come to a genuine heartfelt identification with the poor and suffering? How could I come to her kind of generous and joyful sharing?

She looked at me as though I had asked for a self-evident answer. She explained that it was very easy. I simply had to go to our Lord in the Blessed Sacrament. There I would discover that Jesus becomes bread for us. She said it with great relish, as though she were tasting the most exquisite dish. I, too, should become bread for the poor.

Jesus gave us his own vision of the meaning of human life. What matters in the end is love expressed in action for those in need.

Bread for Us

For the past ten years I have pondered that mysterious answer. Mother Teresa's words continue to reveal treasures of wisdom from the heart of Jesus. Mother Teresa helped me, as she has helped so many others, to know the joy of life as Jesus knows it and to know it within the concrete circumstances of my own situation.

Did I know anyone who had become bread for others? Anyone who was there every day, ready to be "eaten up," giving time, energy, service day after day for love, and enjoying it? I thought immediately of my own parents, of my father's long hours of work, especially during the hard times of the Depression in the 1930s, and of my mother's attention to the details of homemaking, day after day, year after year, for five children and my father. Surely my parents had become bread for us, even as they lovingly provided it.

Memories are deeply nourishing. Many of my favorite memories revolve around meals. Sunday dinners were special events in our house, partly because my mother saved her best recipes for that day, but even more because we took time to be together, sharing the good feeling of belonging to each other. Looking back, I realize what a profound role food plays in our lives. It is much more than physical nourishment. How we deal with food truly tells us how we value others, how we are growing in love at every stage of our lives.

The Ravages of Hunger

There is more to food and hunger, however, than all this goodness. For roughly one out of every seven persons alive today, hunger is not a life-giving signal. It is the occasion of a beautiful experience of God's love and human companionship. Hunger for the desperate poor, many of them small children, is an agonizing experience, an unsatisfied craving that will lead to illness and, for many, to death. For these hundreds of millions of our brothers and sisters, each of whom is Jesus in his most distressing disguise, hunger takes cruel and destructive forms. It is the shriveled limbs and swollen bellies of starving children. Each day on this beautiful planet of ours over forty thousand children, age five years and under, die of malnutrition-related illnesses. That adds up to over fourteen million lives a year. We need to come to terms with the fact that these children are not killed by a disease for which science has found no cure. No, these children are the victims of moral and political failure to see that every person has the basic necessities of life. The poverty-induced hunger rampant in our world today is, to use the words of Pope Paul VI, "an insult flung in the very face of God."

Hunger also means grief of parents, the degradation of picking through garbage cans outside fast-food places and supermarkets in American cities. For many elderly people, in winter the choice is between food and fuel. In Asia, hunger means blindness. Each year hundreds of thousands of persons go blind for lack of a single nutrient, Vitamin A.

All this is going on in a world that spends, annually, more and more billions of dollars for weapons, so that now we have more TNT than food for every person on earth. Is it any wonder that, in 1964, Pope Paul VI urged governments to decrease their weapons budgets in order to put more resources into agricultural development projects? It is a plea that has been repeated many times. Governments find it easy to ignore church leaders when they make this plea. Governments would not be able to ignore the voters, however, if we made our legislators know that we hold them accountable for the way they deal with issues of hunger.

It is painful to think of the complex realities of hunger, but think we must. And we must always ground our thinking in the stark fact that we are dealing with an issue of life and death for real persons. Hunger may be a statistic, but hungry people are not. They suffer and die individually, one by one. We must never let hunger become an abstraction, a way of escaping from hungry people who suffer and die because they are poor. Jesus identifies with each and every one of our brothers and sisters. He has told us that our own eternal salvation depends on how we respond to him in this identification.

We Can Make a Difference

Hunger, in its stark and highly visible forms, touches a chord in us because our own bodies, our own experience, enable us to relate in some way to the hungry. Our experience of God's goodness in our own lives, and in so much that we know of his goodness to others, equally convinces us that we are not doomed to sit by helplessly while we watch our hungry sisters and brothers die. Hunger, like the poverty which causes it, is not inevitable. *We can make a difference.* We can know a joy God intends for us — that of being both host and guest at the banquet of life.

Hunger means grief of parents, the degradation of picking through garbage cans outside fast-food places and supermarkets in American cities. For many elderly people, in winter the choice is between food and fuel.

Thanks to the marvels of modern communication, we know what people are going through in all parts of the world. We do not have to sit and wring our hands. We can become bread for others in a down-to-earth, effective manner, and we can find joy in the process.

There is no special virtue in making ourselves miserable when we can and should be experiencing the joy of sharing in God's concern for his children. Of course, we will have to resist the drag toward selfishness, but we already know that unselfishness and joy go hand in hand. Let me illustrate with a true story.

Recently, I spent a week in a parish that had "soup suppers" on Friday nights during Lent. Each Friday, entire families gathered in the parish hall to have soup and crackers, along with some kind of after-supper discussion for those who cared to stay. Some people brought kettles of soup, which meant that there was a coordinator and committee behind the scenes, of course. But it was very simple, and the atmosphere was one of unmistakable relaxation and happiness. Many people were clearly enjoying themselves.

I found a place next to a retired couple and found it easy to get into conversation. They told me they looked forward to having dinner together with their neighbors once a week. The wife said she especially enjoyed not having to cook that night. Meanwhile, some of the children who had already finished their supper were playing in the large hall and out in the corridor. A few teenagers were watching the children. After the supper we rearranged the chairs for my talk and discussion. About fifty people stayed.

I knew that the people of this parish had started the suppers as a way of helping the hungry. They invited the people who came to give the money they saved to a collection which was divided between the local food pantry and an agency that sent help to the poor in other parts of the world.

In the "soup supper" experience the people of this parish had discovered some precious fringe benefits, not the least of which was a growing experience of community. It also began to occur to them that they could tie some of the parish committee work to the soup suppers. It wasn't necessary to invite an outside speaker each time. In fact, it wasn't necessary to have anything beyond the supper itself. I asked the people why they were going to stop the suppers after Lent, since they obviously enjoyed them so much even while they were also filling a very real need.

This happy parish success story depended on one person taking the initiative, a person like you and me. It is both sobering and exciting to face the fact that a single individual can start an action that can mean life rather than death for hundreds of others. We do not have to dash in front of an automobile to snatch a child from death. We can save lives much more easily. Consider the consequences of the following four ways of responding to the hungry.

First Response: Pray

We can bring our hungry brothers and sisters into our prayer. Instead of simply mentioning the hungry and forgetting them immediately, we can ask Jesus for the grace to see the mystery of food and hunger, feasting and fasting, through his eyes. There is hardly a page of the Gospel which does not have something to say about Jesus and food. The feeding of the multitude, the story of the Good Samaritan, the parable of the rich man and Lazarus, and many other passages of the Gospel witness to the central place eating plays in God's own design. In the deepest mystery of all, the Eucharist, it is bread and wine which unite us to God and to each other in an intimate way that words express only feebly. The stories of Jesus' apparitions after his Resurrection show Jesus preparing breakfast on the beach for his disciples and, on another occasion, revealing himself to two weary disciples who prevailed upon him to stay with them for supper. Luke tells us that their eyes were opened and they knew him in the breaking of bread. (Read Mark 6:30-44 and Mark 8:1-10; Luke 10:29-37, Luke 16:19-31, Luke 24:13-43; and John 21:1-14.)

It is both sobering and exciting to face the fact that a single individual can start an action that can mean life rather than death for hundreds of others.

Once we learn to make food and hunger a part of our prayer, we can find ourselves being joyful and creative in our response to hungry people. Prayer is a way of expressing our own deepest hunger, a hunger for intimacy with God. Prayer is also a way of satisfying that hunger. The psalmist sings of God as a feast for the soul.

If we take time during prayer to reflect on what is happening when we eat, we come to realize that *each time we accept food we are accepting God's love.* God is continuing to create us, providing the very means of our ongoing life through the fruit of the earth and the work of human hands. Praying about food in this way can help us be faithful to the practice of grace before and after meals.

Prayer can transform the way we see hungry people in relation to ourselves. It can bring us to recognize our vocation to share in God's own creative and provident love. Prayer will help us realize, too, that feeding the hungry is a matter of strict justice. The hungry have a right to what they need for life. If we fall into a way of condescending behavior toward the poor, into subtle ways of thinking that we are going beyond the call of justice, we are deceiving ourselves and have not yet seen hunger through the eyes of our Lord. Pope Saint Gregory the Great, who managed a famine relief program in the seventh century, once wrote:

> *Feed the man dying of hunger, for if you have not fed him, you have killed him.*

These strong words found their way into the first code of Church law and, much later, into the Second Vatican Council's Pastoral Constitution on the Church in the Modern World.

Second Response: Learn and Act

We can take the steps to learn about hunger in our own parish and neighborhood; and then we can respond to it. We will almost certainly have to join with others to provide whatever is needed:

organizing a food pantry, perhaps; arranging grocery shopping trips for the elderly; sponsoring a refugee family.

Responding to the hungry may mean inviting a lonely parishioner for dinner in our own home once a week or training teenagers to cook and dine periodically with a widowed member of the parish.

No matter where we live, there are people who are hungry for food and companionship. Christians ought to be keen on satisfying both hungers together. If our parish finds its deepest meaning in the Eucharist celebrated each Sunday, we cannot allow hunger to go unattended. If we turn away from the hungry by our actions, we deny what we profess. The New Testament writing, Acts of the Apostles, makes clear that the first Christians understood this well.

> *They went as a body to the Temple every day but met in their houses for the breaking of bread; they shared their food gladly and generously; they praised God and were looked up to by everyone. Day by day the Lord added to their community those destined to be saved.* (Acts 2:46-47)

Each time we accept food we are accepting God's love. God is continuing to create us through the fruit of the earth and the work of human hands.

We can link our Friday fast and abstinence with our concern for hungry people. Friday abstinence is making a comeback in the Church! In their 1983 pastoral letter, *The Challenge of Peace,* the Catholic bishops of the United States call on all of us to deepen our prayer and penance for peace. The bishops have publicly committed themselves to fast and abstain from meat on all Fridays of the year. They urge us to join them and to add almsgiving to our penance.

Unlike the former Friday abstinence, this is not an obligation. It is, however, strongly urged, and it is encouraging to have our bishops lead the way by their example.

For many Catholics this will mean a return to a practice that gave us one small way of expressing our love and gratitude for our Lord's suffering and dying for us. For younger Catholics it will be a brand new experience. For all of us this penance can also express our determination to respond to the hungry. It will do this if we give the money we save to some group or program working for justice for the poor, as described in the following response.

Third Response: Reach Out

We can reach the hungry across the country and around the world. There are several national Catholic organizations that we can confidently support as we search for ways to respond to the hungry.

One organization, the Campaign for Human Development (CHD), gives funds to projects for economic betterment in the United States. The funds are given on condition that the poor themselves have a strong voice in running the projects. Funds come from an annual fall collection in parishes throughout the country. Each diocese has a CHD director. When Pope John Paul II visited the United States in 1979, he praised the Campaign for Human Development, saying:

> *The efforts aimed at establishing self-help projects deserve praise and encouragement, for in this way an effective contribution is made to removing the causes and not merely the evil effects of injustice. The projects assisted by the Campaign have helped to create a more human and just social order, and they enable many people to achieve an increased measure of rightful self-reliance. They remain in the life of the Church a witness to the love and concern of our Lord Jesus Christ.*

A second organization is Catholic Relief Services (CRS), the official overseas relief and development agency of the Church in this country. CRS began working with victims of World War II and now has programs in many developing countries throughout the world. CRS serves in areas of natural disasters and also in long-range development projects. It puts special emphasis on helping the rural poor improve their economy. Like the Campaign for Human Development, CRS has a director in each diocese and is supported by an annual collection held in parishes throughout the country during Lent.

Fourth Response: Influence Government Policy

We can influence government policy on behalf of hungry people. To have maximum effectiveness in responding to hungry people, we need to face up to the complexities of hunger in today's world economy. Only when we get to the cause of poverty are we touching hunger at its source. We need to find ways to influence public policy in such matters as full employment, trade, debt structure, farm policy, and yes, defense. In 1976, a Vatican statement asserted that the arms race is an act of aggression against the poor because of the high cost:

> *It is an act of aggression which amounts to a crime, for even when armaments are not used, by their cost alone, they kill the poor by causing them to starve.*

Alone, you and I have little chance of influencing public policy in favor of the hungry. This is an area where working together is essential. We need collective action supported by careful analysis and understanding of the political issues and how they can be translated into legislation.

In 1974 there began an ecumenical Christian citizens' movement, on behalf of the hungry, called Bread for the World. A Catholic bishop currently heads the board of directors. A Lutheran minister heads the staff in Washington. Well over 40,000 members of this organization are kept informed of issues in Congress which affect hungry people. Bread for the World is organized along U.S. congressional district and state lines and instructs its members in effective ways to influence their legislators. It is a genuine citizens' lobby on behalf of the hungry, working on both domestic and global issues. It has a good track record for getting legislation passed and has won the respect of many U.S. congresspersons and senators of both major parties.

No matter where we live, there are people who are hungry for food and companionship. If we turn away from the hungry by our actions, we deny what we profess in the Eucharist.

I like to tell a true story from my experience in India which illustrates how important political action is. I had made a trip to a rural mission to visit a former student who was now superior of the community of Sisters there. When I arrived, the Sisters had just made a painful decision to shorten the school year and send the children back to their villages. The reason was simple: United States food aid, on which the school depended, had been cut off. It took a single act of Congress to do this.

The children who were being sent home were not lazy, and they most certainly were not old enough to grow their own food, even if economic and geographic conditions had made this possible. These children were victims of a three-year drought, and their desperate parents were out looking for work while the Sisters took care of the children.

The day after the decision to close the school early, the pastor returned from a tour of the surrounding villages. He said that the mission would need to *extend* the school year because the children would starve if sent back to the villages.

It is idle in a case like this to say that the Indian government should have handled the problem. Lives hung in the balance while the question was debated, and one of the life-giving responses *could* have come from the United States. What we need are legislators called to account by their constituents to make their decisions in light of the basic human needs of real people. Once this principle is followed consistently, many other problems fall into place.

Conclusion

I have described four ways in which we can respond to our hungry brothers and sisters, those with whom our Lord identifies. We will find ourselves acting sometimes more in one way, at other times more in another way, depending on our circumstances. From time to time we should reexamine all four levels of response. We should look for ways to be creative, as were the inventors of the parish soup suppers described earlier.

Only when we get to the cause of poverty are we touching hunger at its source. In 1976 a Vatican statement said of the arms race: *"It is an act of aggression which amounts to a crime, for even when armaments are not used, by their cost alone, they kill the poor by causing them to starve."*

Each step we take will lead to another; if we respond generously, we are almost bound to make a discovery about the meaning of community and the meaning of our own Christian lives. We will find ourselves brought more deeply into communion with others who, like us, long to respond effectively to Jesus in the persons of those who suffer. Struggling for justice, for the kingdom of God, will enrich our own lives in ways we never dreamed. Jesus had a parable about that, too.

> *See that you are dressed for action and have your lamps lit. Be like men waiting for their master to return from the wedding feast, ready to open the door as soon as he comes and knocks. Happy those servants whom the master finds awake when he comes. I tell you solemnly, he will put on an apron, sit them down at table and wait on them.* (Luke 12:35-37)

Now it is our turn to respond to our Lord in those who suffer. One day it will be his turn to share his table with us forever.

Points for Discussion

1. From TV reports and other sources of information, discuss (a) hunger in East Africa and other Third World areas; (b) hunger in our own country; (c) hunger in our own local area. Be as detailed as possible.

2. Using the New Testament passages mentioned in this chapter, and other biblical passages you are familiar with, develop a "Christian Charter" about (a) God's love for us and (b) the poor and basic human justice.

3. In turn, explore each of the four Responses in this chapter. For each Response, formulate a concrete action that is within your capability.

Recommended Reading

Bread for the World by Arthur Simon. Paulist Press and Wm. B. Eerdmans Publishing Company. Revised edition, 1984. Paperback. The author is Executive Director of Bread for the World.

Hunger for Justice: The Politics of Food and Faith by Jack A. Nelson. Orbis Books, 1980. Paperback. This book blends biblical themes with analysis that shows the roots of world hunger in the economic and military policies of the U.S. and other rich nations.

Rich Christians in an Age of Hunger: A Biblical Study by Ronald Sider. Inter-Varsity Press, 1977. Paperback. A very persuasive presentation of the biblical case against hunger.

Index

Fellowship of Reconciliation, 85
Francis of Assisi, St., 78, 97; Peace Prayer of, 78, 97

G

Galbraith, John Kenneth, 102
Gandhi, Mahatma, 77, 97
genocide, 15, 106
good, common, 44
Gregory the Great, Pope St., 117

H

Hiroshima and Nagasaki, atomic bombing of, 13, 50, 55, 66, 107
homelessness, refugees, 32, 105
hunger, starvation, 32, 111-124

I

ideology, ideological differences, 43, 44
illiterates, literacy, 29, 107
Isaiah, Book of, 26

J

Japan, Japanese, 102-103
Jesus, *passim;* teaching of, 22-34
jobs, livelihood: careers, vocations of the young, 94-95; in weapons (defense) industry, 58, 65, 82-83, 103
John, Gospel of, 25, 26, 73-74, 116
John Paul II, Pope, 51, 119; address at Coventry Cathedral, 45, 57, 63, 78; address at Drogheda, Ireland, 38-39; address at Hiroshima, 36-37, 57, 75; address to Pontifical Academy of Sciences (1983), 94, 108; address to U.N. General Assembly (1979), 40-41, 44-45; 1979 World Day of Peace Message — "To Reach Peace, Teach Peace," 37, 48, 56, 81; 1980 World Day of Peace Message — "Truth, the Power of Peace," 39, 40; 1982 World Day of Peace Message — "Peace: A Gift Entrusted to Us," 21, 41-42, 46, 83; 1983 World Day of Peace Message — "Dialogue: The Peacemaker's Task," 42-43, 46-47; peace doctrine of, 35-49, 56-57
John XXIII, Pope, 51, 52-53
justice, 74; economic, 43-44
just-war principles, teaching, 29, 45, 54, 58, 59, 60

K

King, Martin Luther, Jr., 24, 77, 97; "I Have a Dream" speech of, 24, 77
kingdom (reign) of God, 24, 59, 60, 123

L

Last (Final) Judgment, 111
love: of enemies, 28-31, 32; unconditional, 27, 83
Luke, Gospel of, 23, 24, 25, 26, 28, 29, 99, 116, 123

M

Mark, Gospel of, 24, 116
Matthew, Gospel of, 23, 27, 74, 87, 99, 111
Mayeroff, Milton, 81
McSorley, Richard, S.J., 14
militarization, 105
moral judgment, choice, about-face, 37, 45
Mother Teresa of Calcutta, 77, 111-112

violence: as a lie, 38-39; fatalism about, inevitability of, 38, 39; logic of, 40; of war, 20, 21, 36

W

war, warfare: as indiscriminate killing, 53, 89; as least effective way to settle conflicts, 21, 42; as unnecessary evil, 21; bacteriological, 42; conventional, 47; modern, 45-46; nuclear, 42, 47; nuclear as "winnable," 60; total, 59; unacceptability of, 45

weapons (bombs, missiles): atomic, 51; bilateral deep cuts in arsenals of, 62; first strike with nuclear, 62; first use of nuclear, 61; halt in testing, production, deployment of, 62; nuclear, 40, 50, 60; removal from areas likely to be overrun, 62; superiority in, 61

Works of Mercy, of Peace, 28, 32, 92-93

World Military and Social Expenditures (by Ruth Leger Sivard), 104, 110